Praise for ABCs of Raisi~~~

"Such reassuring, solid wisdom in every letter! Dr. Foster's ABCs of Raising Smarter Kids *is a joyful journey through the countless ways parents can help children appreciate their unique strengths and nurture their highest potential. All this, along with the imaginative illustrations by Christine Thammavongsa. It's truly a gift for parents and children alike."*

Mona Delahooke, Ph.D., Author of *Beyond Behaviors: Using Brain Science and Compassion to Understand and Solve Children's Behavioral Challenges*

*"*ABCs of Raising Smarter Kids *provides insightful strategies and resources to help parents foster children's intelligence and nurture core strengths like creativity, resilience, and curiosity. An easy-to-read, comprehensive and well-researched book, parents will find hundreds of ways to inspire every child."*

Marilyn Price-Mitchell, Ph.D., Developmental Psychologist, Roots of Action

*"*ABCs of Raising Smarter Kids *provides guidance to address a breadth of important topics for parents which can be the opening for deeper conversations about dynamics in the home or issues at school or with peers. The appealing format and illustrations also make this a perfect read while waiting in the carpool line, sitting at a music or athletic lesson, or during that quiet time after everyone has gone off to sleep."*

Jennifer L. Jolly, Ph.D., Professor of Gifted Education, University of Alabama; Editor, *Journal for the Education of the Gifted*

"A treasure trove of domains for parents to draw from for the development of their child or adolescent. In this day and age of inclusion and mainstreaming when teachers are stressed out and overwhelmed, this is a sorely needed book—one that teachers can quickly suggest to ALL parents to help in their child's development, and to enhance children's personalities, aptitudes, and potential.

Michael F. Shaughnessy, Ph.D., Professor of Education, Eastern New Mexico University USA; Editor, *Gifted Education International*

"Joanne Foster addresses many of the questions that parents ask about giftedness and its development. She provides brief practical definitions and descriptions of relevant concepts, addressing parents' worries and interests, and informing their decisions. The writing is light-hearted and accessible, and will stimulate parents' enthusiasm and optimism, as it helps them cope with the complex challenges of raising smarter kids. Christine Thammavongsa's surprising and delightful illustrations add another layer of imagination to this book."

Dona Matthews, Ph.D., Psychoeducational Consultant,
Award-winning Author, and Gifted Education Expert

"As a therapist for gifted children and adolescents, I am always looking for the finest resources to pass on to their parents. Joanne Foster's ABCs of Raising Smarter Kids is that perfect resource. From the amazingly, awesome alliteration to the entertaining witticisms, this book is full of wisdom—including timeless quotes, and current books and online resources to aid parents in raising their bright and challenging children."

Lori Comallie-Caplan, MA, LMSW, LED, Counselor,
Coach and Consultant for the Gifted;
Parenting Coordinator and Family Law Mediator

"ABCs of Raising Smarter Kids is an excellent first book for parents—or anyone—with hundreds of questions about how to support the bright children in their care. One of the features I like best is how Dr. Foster introduces a topic and then gives current references for follow-up information in further detail. I confidently recommend this easy-to-read, delightful book!"

Deborah Ruf, Ph.D., Gifted Education Expert and Award-winning Author

"Joanne Foster's latest book is so jam-packed with bite sized information that one could devote an entire school year to applying each helpful idea, one day at a time, and still not run out of new approaches and opportunities to raise smarter kids!"

Sara Dimerman, Psychologist/Author

"Joanne Foster's latest book is a treasure trove. Reach in, choose a page, and come out with golden nuggets each and every time. You can read this book from start to finish, or choose your letter for instantaneous ideas and assistance. An amazing resource."

Lisa Sansom, Coach, Consultant,
Master of Applied Positive Psychology (MAPP)

ABCs of
Raising Smarter Kids

Hundreds of Ways
to Inspire Your Child

What sparks a child's imagination and intellectual growth?
Choice. Encouragement. Guidance. Self-confidence.
Lots of opportunities to think, communicate, explore, and create.
And, letting children's fire or passion come from within.

Step away from the blaze—but from time to time,
celebrate the sizzle, and help fan the flames…

ABCs of
Raising Smarter Kids

Hundreds of Ways
to Inspire Your Child

By Joanne Foster, Ed.D.

Illustrated by
Christine Thammavongsa

ABCs of Raising Smarter Kids

Edited by: Molly A. Isaacs-McLeod
Interior design: The Printed Page
Illustrations: Christine Thammavongsa

Published by
Gifted Unlimited, LLC
12340 U.S. Highway 42, No. 453
Goshen, KY 40025-0966
www.giftedunlimitedllc.com

© 2019 by Joanne Foster

ISBN: 978-1-7337758-0-9

Printed and bound in the United States of America using partially recycled paper.

Gifted Unlimited and associated logos are trademarks and/or registered trademarks of Gifted Unlimited.

At the time of this book's publication, all facts and figures cited are the most current available. All telephone numbers, addresses, and website URLs are accurate and active; all publications, organizations, websites, and other resources exist as described in this book; and all have been verified as of the time this book went to press. The author(s) and Gifted Unlimited make no warranty or guarantee concerning the information and materials given out by organizations or content found at websites, and we are not responsible for any changes that occur after this book's publication. If you find an error or believe that a resource listed here is not as described, please contact Gifted Unlimited.

Much of this material first appeared in *Parenting for High Potential*, an award-winning publication of the National Association for Gifted Children (NAGC), Washington, DC. Originally published as a series of articles featured from June, 2011 through August, 2015, I have since edited the content, significantly updating and supplementing it for publication here. The ABC sketches have been created for this book by Christine Thammavongsa (who, coincidentally, also serves as President of the Board of Directors of ABC Ontario—the Association for Bright Children). We encourage you and your children to unleash your creativity and to color in the illustrations to make the book even more unique. For additional information about the many themes within this book, please check out the numerous resources noted in the bibliography, and the dozens of links in the endnotes—and also the material on my website at www.joannefoster.ca.

Dedications

This book is dedicated to Cara, Allie, Jake, Sari, and Cooper.
May your world be full of wonder and endless possibilities,
and may curiosity guide you toward exciting learning experiences—from A to Z.
J.F.

For Tanisha, Kim, Kevin,
Mary, Tony, Mariah,
Thomas, Malissa, Monica,
Jeffrey, Jimmy, Amanda,
Joshua, Lucas, Ryan,
Emily, Amanda, Jane and Holly.
And for each and every remarkable young person
I have had the pleasure to meet during this life journey.
Knowing you has taught me life's essential lessons from A to Z.
C.T.

Table of Contents:
A "Letter Guide" for Parents

Introduction

A is for alphabetical—and for alliteration.

Moving from **A** through **Z**, I discuss how to encourage and support children's and teens' gifted/high-level development. It is, quite frankly, a "letter way" to share understandings and ideas with parents and teachers. (And kids, too.)

This book is about parenting for intelligence, AND intelligent parenting. My magazine series "ABCs of Being Smart" has come and gone, but the many and diverse needs of high-ability learners have not. Therefore, the messages I conveyed—and which I revisit, hone, extend, and update extensively here—are still very relevant. I welcome the opportunity to connect with a new and enthusiastic cadre of parents and other adults who are seeking information, reassurance, and strategies for raising children.

Indeed, the time is ripe to consider with greater refinement and depth how to develop better educational programs, advocate for change where needed, clarify terms, make meaningful connections, share perspectives, applaud diversity, build cohesive plans, and turn visions into realities. The material in this book will resonate for parents of gifted/high-ability learners, and for the learners themselves. It will also benefit teachers, mentors, would-be educators enrolled in college education programs, coaches, grandparents, and others who want to learn how to nurture children's intelligence and well-being. Parents and teachers of *all* students will discover an organized compilation consisting of hundreds of strategies to help kids aspire to be the best they can be—and then attain those aspirations!

Throughout these pages I present material on a collection of important topics that I also address variously elsewhere, including within my other books, the award-winning *Being Smart about Gifted Education,* and *Beyond Intelligence* (both co-authored with Dona Matthews), as well as *Not Now, Maybe Later* and *Bust Your BUTS* (a 2018 Silver Benjamin Franklin Award winner). Moreover, I offer information and tips culled from a variety of other reliable sources, I include lots of references and resources, and I provide loads of endnote links to valuable websites and online articles. Plus, I draw from my own expertise, reflective of over 30 years of proactive, professional experience as an educator, university course instructor, and gifted education consultant who has worked to facilitate and reinforce children's development.

Within this ABC book, each letter of the alphabet serves as a catalyst for a clear thematic emphasis. I use point form beneath categorical subheadings, often prefaced and complemented by brief, directly targeted narrative segments subtitled "What Matters." Most chapters are formatted in this manner, although a few are structured differently, such as I, K, J, P, Q, and W. Chapters can be read in any order. Some are quite long, whereas others are short—but all are strategically focused. Together they form an informative, reader-friendly resource. There is no tangled jargon. The ABC format is straight-forward; the over-arching themes are pertinent; the content is arranged sensibly; and above all, it is meaningful. The delightful illustrations by Christine Thammavongsa creatively highlight different ideas throughout the book.

I invite parents, teachers, children, and teens to contact me, and to share their questions, concerns, and viewpoints. I look forward to discovering what people have to say, and to learning from their interesting, authentic, and varied experiences. I hope readers will enjoy the unique format of this ABC book, and find the content to be **a**pplicable, **b**eneficial, **c**omprehensive, and more. After **A**, the **B** goes on… And then we'll **C**…

Joanne Foster, Ed.D., July, 2019
www.joannefoster.ca

A is for Awareness
(Also Attunement, Appreciation, Action)

To begin, I've **a**ssembled an **A** list of strategies to **a**ssist parents in becoming more **a**stute. This includes being **a**lert to, **a**ttentive toward, **a**pproachable about, **a**ccommodating of, and **a**dept at handling **a**ssorted gifted-related issues—while taking into **a**ccount children's **a**cademic **a**dvancement. I **a**ddress three **a**reas: 1) ***attunement***, 2) ***appreciation***, and 3) ***action,*** and I present an **a**rray of **a**nnotated **a**pplicable **a**pproaches!

Attunement: What Matters

To ensure children's best possible development at home, school, and elsewhere, parents have to be aware of what's occurring in their children's lives. This includes paying close attention to what they have to say. It involves asking the right kinds of questions, too. For example, instead of asking, *"How was school today?"* you might inquire about their experiences—what they enjoyed doing, seeing, or hearing; what they found challenging; what kindness they observed or participated in; who they met; what they learned in a certain subject area; how they felt about a particular experience; or what they're thinking about investigating further, and why. Parents who find out what makes their child tick—in the classroom, with friends, on the playground, or during sports activities—are better able to support them. And, parents who work toward strengthening communication networks between home and school are also better positioned to help their child succeed. This is because teamwork, respectful conversation, and mutually developed expectations provide a framework wherein everyone is pulling together to benefit the child.

Appreciation: What Matters

Relationships are a foundation for human development, and there are few if any stronger ties than those that exist between a parent and child. It's important for parents to appreciate and be responsive to their child's uniqueness—including passions, personality, concerns, talents, challenges—so as to be able to provide loving care, safety, structure, and guidance. The best nurturing happens in the flow of daily life. And, high levels of academic intelligence do not necessarily mean high levels of emotional or social intelligence. All children need supportive networks and environments to help cope with the variety and complexity of their capacities, the intensity of their feelings, and the intricacies of their social lives. Wise parents understand and appreciate this, and convey belief in their child's ability to navigate the ups and downs, instilling confidence and offering support along the way.

Action: What Matters

When taking action, and in order to make positive change when it's required, it's important to figure out specific and recognizable needs, and then to be practical and realistic about what can be altered. An effective action plan demands thoughtful decision-making and collaborative effort on the part of many people—parents, teachers, administrators, consultants and, of course, the child.

Every home, school, family circle, neighborhood, social milieu, and learning environment has its own particular dynamic and mix of individuals, expectations, advantages, drawbacks, and more. There are many people, of various ages and experiential backgrounds, involved in a child's education and day-to-day life. The compatibility between any one child and the kinds of learning opportunities provided is always in flux, and should be monitored. Parents might have to engage in ongoing decision-making about placement options, gifted programming elements, instruction, or challenge levels. And, taking action might mean that things need to be adjusted a little, or possibly even shaken up a lot, at any one point, or over time.

Listen carefully to what others have to say. Be patient. Pacing, mutual respect, and flexibility are integral. Each community is a complex and interdependent place. Parents who act successfully on behalf of their child know the value of nurturing productive relationships and a climate of trust, and the importance of ongoing attunement to the child in order to ensure academic and other kinds of advancement, and well-being.

Attunement

○ **A**ctive listening and observing—heed what children say and do, and sometimes do *not* say and do. Don't just listen in order to respond. Listen in order to understand.

○ **A**nswer—respond to children's questions about their abilities in ways appropriate to their level of understanding.

○ **A**sk—encourage them to ask more questions.

○ **A**nticipate—be prepared to address issues and matters relating to academic advancement in a timely manner, as they arise. It's not just about *schooling*—consider children's interests, choices, and capabilities.

○ **A**utonomy—respect the child's individualism and desire for independence.

○ **A**vailability—be there—in person, in spirit, indefinitely, and as needed.

○ **A**dapt—help children manage the changes that occur in their lives, including transitions to special programs, new friendships, family circumstances, and various situations that may occur at school or elsewhere.

○ **A**ffective—pay attention to the *whole* person; social, emotional, and motivational development go hand-in-hand with cognitive development, contributing to the overall well-being of the child.

Appreciation

○ **A**cknowledge—encourage children's efforts, not just their accomplishments.

○ **A**spire—help children fuel their imaginations, tackle challenges, stretch the intellect, and set goals that are high but reachable.

○ **A**synchrony—appreciate that any one child often has areas of strength *and* weakness, and that these can develop at different rates and times.

○ **A**cademic**, A**rtistic and **A**thletic **A**bilities—some learners have academic strengths, and others are artistically or athletically inclined and may excel in such areas as drama, music, sculpture, dance, skating, gymnastics, swimming… Encourage and support a range of abilities and pursuits.

○ **A**nti-intellectualism—the term implies resentment, disrespect, or suspicion of people who excel in certain areas. There is certainly no place for these kinds of dispositions among those who recognize the value of having and using intelligence, and striving for excellence.

○ **A**ttitude—parents' attitudes about giftedness and high-level development really do matter. Thoughts and feelings about a child's heightened abilities—and the many possible implications—can range from confusion to anxiety to excitement, with infinite possibilities in between. Parental attitudes will be influenced by the nature and accuracy of the resources they acquire, reflect upon, and apply; the kinds of support they receive; the extent to which they network and share useful information with one another; and also whether they think and act in positive, collaborative, flexible, and constructive ways. (For more on all of this, see my segment "Parental Attitudes" in the *Encyclopaedia of Giftedness, Creativity, and Talent*.[1])

○ **A**lready-mastered material—students who have mastered knowledge should not have to sit in class and bide their time. Above-level testing (noted in the section below) can help to determine what kids have already grasped, and when it's time to up the ante. Parents and teachers can discuss ways to ensure that children are happily engaged and productive.

○ **A**ccountability—allow children to take responsibility for their actions, including chores, homework, task completion, goal-setting, and day-to-day behavior.

Action (at home, school, and in other contexts)

○ **A**rrange—be proactive; help to facilitate learning opportunities, including having discussions with others who can assist in nurturing children's development and success.

○ **A**ccess—find, sift through, read, and use up-to-date and reliable resources. Granted, there is a huge proliferation of resource material "out there" and it can be challenging to zero in on what is most essential to anyone's own particular needs or concerns. Look for current and well-referenced books, articles, podcasts, and videos. Consider, for example, the range of parenting and teaching material on gifted-related issues suggested on Carolyn Kottmeyer's site *Hoagies' Gifted Education Page*.[2] And have a look at the online resources offered through Duke University's Talent Identification Program (TIP).[3]

○ **A**ffluence—you don't have to *be* rich to *en*rich—there are lots of possibilities, with family and friends, online, within the community, and beyond.

○ **A**dministrative support—parents and teachers cannot do it alone! Administrators can have a direct impact on the efficacy of a district's gifted service provisions. Targeted resources on research-based and standards-based practices in gifted education are increasingly available for use by administrators, and by professional development leaders. These materials help to build coherence and ensure educational quality across classrooms, programs, schools, and boards. Administrators can help arrange for coordinated efforts among professionals, strong communication channels with parents, increased professional development in gifted education, additional consultative services, and other supports.

○ **A**ssociations—there are many organizations that parents can join or contact to acquire support and learn how to foster children's high-level development. For example, National Associations for Gifted Children (NAGC in the US, NZAGC in New Zealand, Potential Plus UK in the United Kingdom, and other affiliated associations around the world); the Association for Bright Children (ABC, in Canada); Associations for Gifted and Talented Education (variably state by state in the U.S.[4]); Supporting Emotional Needs of the Gifted (SENG in the U.S. and Europe); and Council for Exceptional Children (CEC).

○ **A**ctivities—there are countless opportunities for learning—in regular classrooms; in special programs at school, or during the summer, holiday times, or on weekends; in extracurricular programs; at home; with mentors; through special interest contests and clubs; and via global and technological means.

○ **A**dvanced placement—cooperative endeavors between secondary schools and the College Board. Students take programs with accelerated content and meet college-level educational objectives during high school. Some colleges and universities grant course credit, or offer placement based on high scores.

○ **A**ptitude—encompassing both cognitive strengths (such as reasoning ability, prior knowledge), and extra-cognitive factors (such as motivation, interest, persistence), aptitude is directly linked to the context in which learning occurs, including kinds of instruction, resources, support systems, technology, and connectivity with different disciplines—all of which influence success.

○ **A**uthentic challenge—tasks should be relevant and connected to individual interests or real-world problems.

○ **A**ssessment—teachers can (and should) find out what a child knows in any one subject area, teaching and building understandings from there, and monitoring and evaluating progress along the way. This is a sure-fire approach to augmented learning. A formal assessment is a comprehensive evaluation of an individual's areas of strength and weakness, using a variety of approaches. These might include tests, questionnaires, observations, inventories, interviews, and reports from other sources. Assessments yield findings and recommendations. Teachers often use formative and summative assessments in class. Formative assessments are in-process monitoring of children's progress and comprehension, whereby teachers can offer feedback and guidance, provide opportunities for further learning, and maximize achievement. Teachers can assess children's progress during the course of schoolwork in many ways, including checking assignments, answers in class, and student engagement—and then plan instruction, and when and how to move ahead. A summative assessment indicates what a student knows at the end of a lesson or a unit of instruction.

○ **A**bove-level testing—this is a good way to find out how much an advanced learner already knows.[5] Grade-level tests provide data about certain skills but may not be indicative of a child's full capabilities because they don't necessarily enable kids to show just how far they've mastered material above that grade. Above-level testing is an option for ascertaining learners' relative strengths—that is, to what extent they are ahead, and how much they know in a particular subject area. Parents and teachers can work together to decide on and employ a comprehensive testing process, using both subjective and objective information from more than one source to develop appropriate strategies for addressing a child's gifted/high-level-ability.

○ **A**cceleration—the goal of acceleration is to move a child ahead toward more satisfying academic involvement. There are many approaches that can be embarked upon in an informed and thoughtful manner, including single-subject and full grade acceleration, telescoping of grades (such as three years across two), and early entrance to programs. For more information on acceleration, see *The Iowa Acceleration Scale, 3rd Edition* by Susan Assouline, Nicholas Colangelo, Ann Lupkowski-Shoplik, Jonathan Lipscomb, and Leslie Forstadt.[6] To learn more about the benefits of acceleration, see *A Nation Empowered* edited by Susan G. Assouline, Nicholas Colangelo, Joyce-Van-Tassel-Baska, and Ann Lupkowski-Shoplik.[7]

○ **A**bility grouping—refers to children working with others who share their capability levels; a more flexible approach is one that encourages mixed grouping and individual pursuits as well.

○ **A**dvocacy—one of the most important **A** words in terms of making a difference for children because advocacy—and self-advocacy on the part of kids—can facilitate, nurture, and support their development. The book *Academic Advocacy for Gifted Children: A Parent's Comprehensive Guide, 3ʳᵈ Edition* by Barbara Gilman offers information and guidance. And, in *The Power of Self-Advocacy for Gifted Learners*, educator and author Deb Douglas focuses on helping students understand their rights and responsibilities; develop their learner profiles, investigate available options and opportunities; and connect with advocates.

○ **A**bsolute—there is no one absolute or sure-fire action plan that will suit or appeal to every parent or child. Learn all you can about how to develop a strong foundation that will support *your* child's growth and well-being. The possibilities range from **A** to **Z**…

Author's Addendum: Additional **A** list suggestions for parents can be found on pages 280-286 of *Being Smart about Gifted Education, 2ⁿᵈ Edition*. These subheadings include **A**ctivities for Rainy (and Not So Rainy) Days; **A**ugmented Learning; **A**ccounting; **A**chievement; **A**utonomy; and there are further ideas on **A**dvocacy as well.

B is for Basics: And the B Goes on...

There are **b**oundless ways to help children **b**uild intelligence, and **b**oost self-confidence, resilience, and strength of character. The **b**asics are: 1) ***Being***, followed by 2) **<u>Doing</u>**, and 3) ***Stretching***!

Basics: What Matters

As a parent, teacher, teacher trainer, gifted education consultant, and author, I've thought and written about giftedness and its development for many decades. I've grappled with gifted learning needs from both personal and professional perspectives—including working with countless teachers and schools in a number of different ways to implement sound practices for gifted learners, and with parents to help them support gifted development in their children. Over the years I've encountered many widespread misconceptions that get in the way of parents and educators fostering and supporting children's gifted development.

What does **Being** gifted mean? Most people would agree that Albert Einstein was a genius. However, he was not a stellar student when he was a youngster. And, this speaks to the fact that children's developmental trajectories, like their potential, are predictably unpredictable. Einstein had highly specialized abilities in some areas, and deficits in others. Even if there had been "gifted testing" back in his day, he probably would not have been nominated. And, it's unlikely that he'd have done exceedingly well on the tests. We'll never know. In any case, tests of intelligence and ability are far more limited than human potential.

Fast forward, and today's researchers are studying neural plasticity. This is a term that refers to the dynamic flexibility and individual variability of brain development. It has important implications for anyone who is interested in gifted development. It suggests that under the right circumstances, exceptional abilities can develop in children who previously would never have been considered for gifted education or advanced learning opportunities. Current research findings on cognitive development—and on the ways in which strengths can emerge in domain specific areas (over time, and with the right supports and opportunities to learn)—are informing and refining understandings of giftedness. It makes more sense to say that people show evidence of gifted-level ability in, say, mathematics, linguistics, or music, rather than categorizing some children as "being gifted," and others as "not gifted." Moreover, the brain is always changing and amenable to learning, so someone's exceptionalities may come to light over time. When it comes to "being gifted" we have to be careful. Being who we are—and striving to be the best we can be—is what really matters. A wise parent and rabbi, Jonathan Berkun, suggests that it makes sense to ask older children and young teens, "*What makes you, you?*" and then "*Who will you be?*" and to encourage their thoughts, individualism, and aspirations. Anyone is apt to shine!

Therefore, **Doing** and **Stretching** also matter—they are the action components—and they can make all the difference in whether or not children thrive. Help children engage their intelligence, creativity, and determination. This will empower them to invest in their own active learning and give them the edge to succeed. "*Give children a strong appreciation for curiosity, exploration, and persistence. This is the foundation upon which intelligence, creativity, success, and fulfilment are built.*" (Excerpted from *Beyond Intelligence*, p. 240)

The points below underscore this point.

Being!

○ **B**rainpower—something to be proud of—every day. Collaborations among researchers, clinicians, educators, and students increasingly show that brain health affects cognitive, physical, and emotional well-being. Brain health can be augmented with smart habits such as exercise, good nutrition, reflection, adequate rest, reading, and meaningful interaction with others. John F. Kennedy said, "*The human mind is our fundamental resource.*" Let's keep it strong.

○ **B**olster children's confidence—help them feel good about themselves, even in areas of weakness, where they can learn to take pride in their efforts, their perseverance, and their improvement.

○ **B**abies—the earliest experiences and relationships are formative, and help little ones develop neural connections, foundational competencies, and interactive skills. The website Zero to Three[8] offers an abundance of valuable information for parents (and teachers, and caregivers, too), with articles and resources to help children flourish throughout the infant and toddler years—with lasting effects for emotional health and lifelong well-being. And, Tracy Cutchlow's book *Zero to Five: 70 Essential Parenting Tips Based on Science* is a colorful, oh-so-easy-to-read book that showcases meaningful moments and highlights practical strategies for use by anyone who lives or works with small children. (Bravo to photographer Betty Udesen for the beautiful pictures!)

○ **B**ored—when children are not sufficiently challenged they often become bored and frustrated—and who can blame them?

○ **B**ored (again…)—and then, sometimes being bored is the best way to figure out what one really wants to learn and do.

○ **B**ored (still…)—help children get busy with something they're interested in or curious about!

○ **B**enevolence—aside from academics, parents and teachers can help children become kind, compassionate, and contributing members of society.

○ **B**etter—remember: gifted learners are not better than others; they're just following their own developmental pathways.

○ **B**elonging (rejection can be brutal)—social competence varies from child to child, and it has little to do with academic competence. Caring adults can assist children in finding that friendly fit, or a fitting friend, by talking to kids honestly about their giftedness, and their concerns about relationships, social norms, and how to build and maintain friendships. For more information on this, see Dr. Eileen Kennedy-Moore's book for children, *Growing Friendships: A Kids' Guide to Making and Keeping Friends*.

○ **B**alance—personal balance involves juggling the challenges of daily life in healthy ways and learning to accept what's difficult alongside that which is easy.

○ **B**elieve in children—convey that belief, and they will learn to believe in themselves.

Doing!

○ **B**eing smart is just the beginning—actually doing something with one's capabilities, and putting forth effort, is a lot more important. *"Intelligence is the dynamic interplay of engagement and ability in pursuit of personal goals."* Those words, by noted researcher and author Scott Barry Kaufman, emphasize how doing (that is, being proactive), is integral to intelligence-building.

○ **B**oasting—sometimes *"showing your knowing"* can be perceived by others as boastful or arrogant. Children should be encouraged to share their ideas and understandings with pride, but in ways that don't eclipse others.

○ **B**ragging—*"My son is soooo smart he can count backwards by threes from 1000. Want to hear?"* Be proud, not inconsiderate. Pleasant, not pompous.

○ **B**est practice in gifted education—there are so many models of instruction and approaches to teaching that it's next to impossible to label any one as the best practice. Find out what works most effectively for each student in response to individual needs, nuances, and circumstances. An Individual Education Plan (IEP) or sometimes a Gifted Educational Plan (GIP) with specific recommendations may be devised by the school team working on behalf of the child.

○ **B**usy work (versus meaningful activities)—know the difference. Then think about and act upon it.

○ **B**ehavioral problems—when learning is pleasurable, motivating, and successful, children are less likely to act out. However, when they feel frustrated, angry, disillusioned, or experience other negative emotions, then it's important to think about the possible underlying reasons for their misbehavior, and to employ responsive, and preventive strategies. Two cautionary notes: Learning problems can contribute to negative behavior so be sure to consider that possibility. And secondly, when behavior is seriously concerning—hostile, persistently disruptive, or when children consistently ignore major age-appropriate societal standards—it's time to seek professional help. Mona Delahooke is a paediatric psychologist, and her blog offers helpful articles on dealing with behavioral issues.[9] Her newest book *Beyond Behaviors: Using Brain Science and Compassion to Understand and Solve Children's Behavioral Challenges,* is very informative, and contains strategies, worksheets, and resources. Also, the non-profit organization Lives in the Balance has a website with online resources using the "Collaborative and Proactive Solutions" approach to help behaviorally challenging kids.[10]

○ **B**ridge—bridge any gaps between what a child *is* learning in school, and what he *needs* and *wants* to learn…

○ **B**ullying—bullying can take many forms. Aggression may be physical, verbal, written, cyber; bullies and victims may be young or old; and any kind of learner can be targeted. Bullying behaviors have to be addressed and eradicated in a sensitive, timely, informed manner by teachers, parents, and students, working together. Resources for parents—including strategies, training materials, questions and answers—are available through regional education centers, school portals, community health outlets, help lines, regional police stations, and various other local organizations and programs, most of which are accessible online. A superb resource is Michele Borba's book *End Peer Cruelty, Build Empathy: The Proven 6 Rs of Bullying Prevention that Create Inclusive, Safe, and Caring Schools.* The author focuses on respectful relationships, and on how to make lasting change. (The 6 Rs are rules, recognize, report, respond, refuse, and replace.) And, there is information on how to teach kids to identify and safely stand up to bullying through websites that are offered by government agencies.[11]

○ **B**ooks—Read. Enjoy reading. Read lots. Read together. Read aloud. Encourage children to read. It will enhance their understandings of people, places, and things; increase their vocabulary, and provide portals into new realms. See *Some of My Best Friends Are Books, 3ʳᵈ Edition* by Judith Wynn Halsted for an annotated bibliography of over 300 books that promote children's intellectual and emotional well-being.

Stretching!

○ **B**eyond the curriculum—seek out the atypical. Give children choice and explore various kinds of activities within and outside your community.

○ **B**udding—growth is ongoing, as is learning—and must be nurtured with continual support that is both sensitive and responsive to individual needs.

○ **B**roaden understandings—of giftedness and high-level development. How can parents do that? See the next bullet point. And, the one after that. And, others throughout this book…

○ **B**uild networks of support—in such areas as advocacy, instructional methods, resource sharing, and anything else that has an impact on a child's learning and healthy development. Get to know people. Make alliances. Ponder different points of view. Integrate perspectives. Stay in the loop.

○ **B**ring new ideas to the table—connect creative applications to educators' teaching and learning, to professional development, to counseling and guidance processes, and to any approaches that might stimulate children's learning.

○ **B**rain-based research—scientific studies in areas such as cognitive neuroscience continue to inform education and have an impact on parenting, teaching, and learning. Consider finding out more! *The Whole Brain Child: 12 Revolutionary Strategies to Nurture Your Child's Developing Mind* by Daniel J. Siegel and Tina Payne Bryson, is a very readable and interesting resource that parents will want to refer to often. The authors describe how the brain works, how it matures, and how to nurture healthy brain development. Kids can also learn about how the brain works—have a look at the *Brainology* program.[12]

○ **B**uzz—create and discover websites, conferences, people, webinars, podcasts, journal articles, workshops… There are countless resources to tap. Share the information.

○ **B**readth—help kids learn to ask pertinent questions. Indira Ghandi said, "*The power to question is the basis for all human progress.*" Increasing the scope and sophistication of inquiry will enable children to extend their understandings, and learn at a higher, broader, and deeper level.

C is for Clarifying Complexities (I Can C Clearly Now)

> Here I concentrate on the letter **C**, and categorize and crystallize concepts concerning some complexities of raising smarter kids. Central points are: 1) *capabilities*, 2) *connections*, and 3) *crucial considerations*.

Capabilities, Connections, and Considerations: What Matters

When it comes to childrearing, parents have different concerns, priorities, and understandings. These are based on personal experiences, acquired knowledge, circumstances, and a whole host of influences and factors.

However, there are many practical strategies parents can use to encourage children to invest in their learning and develop their *capabilities*. Conviction, choice, and challenge are just three examples noted within the bulleted points below.

Connections are also important because they provide links, networks, information, and support. Connectivity comes in many forms.

And, there are some key *considerations* for parents who want to help their children thrive. These include creativity, critical thinking, challenge, courtesy, change, curiosity, compassion, counseling and consultation. Imagine life without the impetus of creative or critical thought. What would the world be like if it was devoid of courtesy, curiosity, and compassion? How would parents manage if they could not acquire counseling, or consult with others during challenging times of change?

All of the above are foundational, regardless of one's parenting style. Here's more on how to cultivate capabilities, develop meaningful connections, and pay attention to core considerations.

Cultivate Capabilities

○ **C**onviction—determination, enthusiasm, and passion are cornerstones of success.

○ **C**hoice—offering children lots of learning opportunities enables them to grow in different directions. Ancient Greek philosopher Pythagorus said, *"Choices are the hinges of destiny."*

○ **C**ompetence—it doesn't just happen; in order to master something people have to work hard, not simply rest on their laurels. Proficiency is developed, not given.

○ **C**ognitive development—children develop at different rates, and there is considerable diversity in the ways in which they learn. A child who exhibits advanced intellectual development may not be as advanced in other areas. Moreover, some kids thrive in a relaxed environment wherein they're given latitude, whereas others do well when rules and expectations are strictly enforced. Sudden bursts in the development of cognitive abilities can occur, as can smooth progression over time. Plus, learning needs and preferences change across a child's development. Cognitive development can unfold in surprising and remarkable directions as kids mature and actively explore their world.

○ **C**omparison—avoid comparing children's abilities, at school or at home. Don't let differences be a source of conflict. Help kids appreciate their own unique strengths, and also how to manage their areas of weakness. In a healthy family environment, everyone feels supported, and values the abilities of others. Different opportunities and activities may be needed for family members at different times, and so parents may have to balance their time, resources, and attention accordingly. A strong family circle is comprised of people who convey appreciation for one another, stay connected, and are respectful of variations in interests, personal attributes and capabilities.

○ **C**haracter education—increasingly, schools are incorporating "character development" programs into the curriculum. Areas of focus include respect, responsibility, empathy, initiative, resilience, reliability, honesty, integrity, fairness, and compassion. Children learn the importance of these virtues when parents and teachers model them, and emphasize their value. See Sara Dimerman's book *How to Influence Your Kids for Good* for more information, and also activities to help strengthen a child's moral compass. And, visit the Roots of Action website to learn more about the "Compass Advantage."[13]

○ **C**ommon sense—not the same thing as intellectual prowess, common sense is something that parents can help children develop through demonstration and consistent guidance. Author Voltaire said, "*Common sense is not so common.*" Let's endeavor to change that.

○ **C**onfidence—not all gifted/high-ability learners are confident in their abilities (academic, social, or other), and some need help with this. There's down-to-earth advice and practical tips in Eileen Kennedy-Moore's book *Kid Confidence: Help Your Child Make Friends, Build Resilience, and Develop Real Self-Esteem.*

○ **C**ontrol—children feel respected when they're given age-appropriate autonomy, and rules are dependably enforced, but somewhat flexible.

○ **C**oping—to help children become more resilient in the face of setbacks, answer their questions, listen to their concerns, allay their fears, assuage their worries, and suggest resources that they can consult when they're upset or apprehensive. Become familiar with the necessary resources yourself so as to ensure that they are appropriate. For example, there's Dan Peters' *Make Your Worrier a Warrior*, with its companion guide for kids, *From Worrier to Warrior*, and the complementary *Warrior Workbook*. Another helpful reference book is *The Fear Fix: Solutions for Every Child's Moments of Worry, Panic, and Fear* by Sarah Chana Radcliffe.

○ **C**ulture—cultural identity and influences have a direct bearing on who we are, and how we learn. Ways of doing things or believing help to define us, and these are passed along through teachings and by learning—often over time, and from one generation to the next. Cultural awareness and affirmation should also be part of a child's classroom experience, with opportunities for students to acknowledge and appreciate cultural diversity.

Connections

○ **C**larification—clarify expectations—your own, the school's, the child's, and others', to ensure that demands are well-defined, fair, and adaptable.

○ **C**ommunication—open channels encourage involvement and strengthen relationships. Communication takes many forms—for example, through art, writing, performance, speaking, and body language. Important communication skills include listening, observing, giving and receiving feedback, and empathizing with others. All of these help children become more adept at learning.

○ **C**ollaboration—working with others is a great way to learn and to achieve goals, and also to create a rich and engaging learning environment for *all* children, at school, and also on the home front. Collaboration begins within the family, and through different interactions as children grow, share, play, and learn how to get along with others. These early lessons cement the foundation for more sophisticated collaborations as kids mature. But perhaps the most important collaboration is the one that occurs between parent and child over the course of many years. Ross Greene's book *Raising Human Beings: Creating a Collaborative Partnership with Your Child* is a close-up look at how to develop a collaborative, and non-adversarial approach to parenting.

○ **C**ontext—the milieu in which people work or play (such as home or school) has a direct impact on levels of accomplishment and motivation, and on attitudes toward learning.

○ **C**ompetitions, **C**ontests, and **C**lubs—activities may range from recreational pastimes to studies or competitions at advanced levels. These extracurricular pursuits enable children to reach out and connect with others who have similar interests. For example, Johns Hopkins Center for Talent Development has an online source for investigating academic competitions.[14] Areas include history, math, science, art, and writing, as well as quiz bowls and multidisciplinary contests. Rivalries can sometimes be strong, however, so parents may have to help children understand the nature of competitive activities, and how to win and lose gracefully.

○ **C**omputers and electronic devices—these are gateways to learning for today and tomorrow—although screen time might need to be limited, and supervision is always critical. This is especially so in the early years. Technology offers many benefits for children and teenagers but it can be problematic if it interferes with their responsibilities, friendships, other activities, family connectivity, school work, sleep, exploration and play, or well-being. Parents can be mindful of all of this, and of what they are demonstrating by way of their own use of technology as well. Much has been written about the risks of distracted parenting due to overuse of cellphones and other electronic devices. There are helpful resources and guidelines for what is sometimes called modern day "technoference" (for people of all ages) available online.[15] And, because online safety is critical, parents have to make a concerted effort to teach children Internet navigation skills and safety. The book *Screenwise: Helping Kids Thrive (and Survive) in the Digital World* by Devorah Heitner is a very helpful resource. Parents can also look for family-friendly search engines that help to control children's online activities through query results selection processes, site restriction, and keyword blocking mechanisms. For example, Kiddle[16] is designed to be a "*kid safe visual search engine*" and it "*filters sites with explicit or deceptive content.*" Parents should be prudent and vigilant, taking the time they need to investigate various options and measures so as to be thorough.

○ **C**o-creating—parents, teachers, and children can and should work cohesively to make learning relevant, and as motivating as possible.

○ **C**ross-grade and **C**ross-curricular learning—encourage teachers to look beyond the regular grade, subject, or classroom curriculum to tap into enriching material.

○ **C**ommunity—a good place to play, learn, and work with others; to develop a sense of self; to volunteer and contribute to the greater good; to make friends; and to acquire lots of neighborhood resources!

Crucial Considerations

○ **C**reativity—encourage children's ideas—even the seemingly outlandish ones—so they can extend their enthusiasms. What can be more exciting than discovery, innovation, and trying something new? Poet Maya Angelou wisely said, "*You can't use up creativity. The more you use, the more you have.*" So use it! For ideas on how to nurture creativity, see the book *Wired to Create: Unraveling the Mysteries of the Creative Mind* by Scott Barry Kaufman and Carolyn Gregoire. The Henry Ford Foundation focuses on teaching innovation, and helping kids develop resourcefulness and ingenuity.[17] Poke through the column "Fostering Kids' Success" at The Creativity Post,[18] and be sure to see the site's homepage for other content on how to stimulate creativity, innovation, and imagination.

○ **C**ritical thinking—every bit as important as creative thinking, and a stepping-stone to reasoned inquiry and sophisticated thought processes. Critical thinking involves various applications such as logical reasoning, learning to discriminate between things, predicting, breaking things down into foundational parts, analyzing, evaluating, making inferences, and questioning. Critical thinking informs judgments, helps people solve problems, and prepares kids to tackle challenges. Being able to think more reflectively, broadly, and astutely are prerequisites for high-level proficiency. Tenacity is also good. Albert Einstein said, "*It's not that I'm so smart. It's just that I stay with problems longer.*"

○ **C**hallenge—the best kind of challenge is one you can master. Not too cushy, not too complex, but at a comfortable level. Sometimes people have to work really hard to get through a challenge and reach that "tadah!" point. Others put creative ideas or critical thinking into practice and try new ways of tackling challenges.

○ **C**ourtesy—be considerate of others when in potentially thorny or delicate situations, such as meetings with teachers and school administrators.

○ **C**ourage—the courage to persevere in the face of difficulty, to ask for help, to be oneself, to take sensible risks, to take a creative leap, to stick with your beliefs… These are just a few examples of what courageousness might entail, and that are at the core of important lessons that children can learn from parents. The Joyful Courage Parenting Podcast[19] features episodes that focus on different topics having to do with supporting, inspiring, and informing parents—who in turn can support, inspire, and inform their children.

○ **C**hange—help children adjust to new programs, friends, challenges, and heightened expectations. Be patient, and also constructive and caring during times of transition.

○ **C**uriosity—stimulate a sense of wonder and inquisitiveness—an effective way to motivate anyone. Author William Arthur Ward said, *"Curiosity is the wick in the candle of learning."* Light the wick!

○ **C**ompassion—children appreciate it when the adults in their world genuinely heed and respect their feelings and concerns. And, everyone benefits.

○ **C**ounseling and **C**onsultation—parents and teachers sometimes require help to understand the exceptional developmental needs of children, and sometimes children experience stressors and also require counseling services. Consult with professionals to explore the range of support systems available in your neighborhood or school district.

○ **C**ongratulations!—on all your efforts, and all you do to support gifted/high-ability learners as they endeavor to set, monitor, and achieve their goals!

D is for Development

Determining what giftedness is all about means directing attention to dimensions of the individual. Here I deal with developmental deliberations, including specifics about giftedness (*details*), and some ways of thinking (*dispositions*).

Development: What Matters

Gifted-level development is not easily categorized. Definitions of giftedness differ broadly. Misinformation and controversy about giftedness abound, and it can be daunting, confusing, and overwhelming—for parents and for children. Learners are not cookie-cutter, and neither are families. Support systems vary, and so do life circumstances and the ways in which they're managed by parents and kids. Child development rests on countless factors.

It's helpful if parents work together with their child's teachers and healthcare professionals, determining needs based on the lived experience of the child, and then building a framework from which to address them. Efforts should rest upon an attitude that conveys respect for individuality and uniqueness, and for the intellectual and other domain-specific abilities of the child. These efforts can be invigorated and made more positive when understandings of high-level-ability and giftedness are clarified, and when parents perceive success as they endeavor to find and acquire suitable educational opportunities for their child's optimal development.

Gifted-level development cannot, and should not, be pigeon-holed. In *Beyond Intelligence* (p. 104), Dona Matthews and I state, "*The important thing for parents to help children understand is that over the years they'll develop a wide range of intelligences, strength of character, and insights that no IQ test could possibly measure, and that no label could ever define.*" Development, and indeed life itself, is not stable. It's about change, learning, and possibility.

Some fundamentals about child development follow here, and these may help to inform parents and others who seek to better understand gifted learners.

Details (about gifted development...)

○ **D**evelopmental **d**ifferences—no two children will have the exact same experiences across their lives. Giftedness is about diversity, and differences in how people develop. It has to do with genetic predispositions, influences, motivation, reflection, hard work, intellectual stimulation, and the kinds of interactions and experiences a person has. People create their own intelligence and develop their abilities over time and across the lifespan.

○ **D**efinition—there is no one universally accepted definition of giftedness. However, giftedness is not passive. It is part of a developmental process and is therefore dependent upon how a person engages with ideas, people, circumstances, environments, and the challenges of daily life. For those who nevertheless want a definition, here's one that Dona Matthews and I discuss more fully in *Being Smart about Gifted Education*, wherein the focus of a gifted designation relates to its practical education implications.

"Giftedness is exceptionally advanced, subject-specific ability at a particular point in time, and in a particular context, such that an individual's educational needs cannot be well met without making significant adaptations to the curriculum or providing other learning opportunities."

○ **D**iversity—individuality is predicated on being oneself—and differences can be related to age, race, socio-economic status, sexual orientation, physical or cognitive abilities, beliefs, and more. Children can be taught that differences are assets, that they can be smart in different ways, and that diversity is a strength.

○ **D**ynamic—growth is fluid, and so a person's capabilities change over time along with their ability to understand ideas, adapt to the environment, overcome difficulties, and learn from experiences.

○ **D**omains—this refers to the contexts in which we live and learn, and also subject-specific areas of strength and weakness. (Like math, languages, sports, music, and so on.)

○ **D**iagnostics—teachers can be "mismatch diagnosticians." That is, they can find out individual students' current educational (and other) needs, and then plan learning and programs accordingly. "Mismatch Diagnostics" is the title of Chapter 3 in *Being Smart about Gifted Education*. That chapter is about how teachers can diagnose learning mismatches. We also address parents' roles in providing valuable information and working collaboratively with teachers to identify children's learning issues, abilities, and accomplishments.

○ **D**ocumentation—it's a good idea to keep a record of your child's accomplishments both in and out of school—along with examples of the kinds of supports that help him or her flourish in different settings.

○ **D**ifferentiation—differentiated programs are teaching practices that offer a flexible range of options, and that focus on the individual student. For a thorough understanding of differentiation in practice, check out the book *The Differentiated Classroom* by Carol Ann Tomlinson. It's a valuable resource for teachers, and an in-depth source of information for parents. Lannie Kanevsky has also researched differentiation and has worked extensively in the field of gifted education. She is part of a team of professionals who provide an informative online resource called Possibilities for Learning that focuses on *"planning for and with highly able learners"*—including offering strategies for differentiating for individual needs.[20] And, The Renzulli Learning System is another option to consider, with a home edition for parents as well.[21]

○ **D**ifficulties—gifted learners may struggle with some tasks. Maybe math, spelling, organization, or sports… Not everything is a slam dunk. Be available to share resources, guidance, reinforcement, and reassurance. Encourage determination.

○ **D**etermination—help kids appreciate that they can become a creator, collaborator, developer, achiever, or dreamer—in short, someone who will turn their curiosity and know-how into something exciting and gratifying. They can accomplish this by working hard and extending their wonder and knowledge, and by linking their ideas to experiences, informational sources, and other modes of thought. But they have to dig in. Determination, resilience, and staying power can facilitate learning, and help make us stronger and wiser. (Who can you think of who has true grit?)

○ **D**ual exceptionalities—sometimes referred to as twice exceptional or 2E, there are many students who have strengths in some areas, alongside one or more disabilities. This can make it difficult to identify the high-level ability. It's vital not to overlook strengths, to address any learning needs, and to support kids as they develop compensatory strategies. This might involve technological approaches, programming adaptations, learning about self-advocacy, getting help with goal-setting, or other means of understanding unique skill sets—and meeting challenges. For information on supporting 2E learners, check out the *2enewsletter*[22] and *TECA—Twice Exceptional Children's Advocacy,*[23] and also Michael Postma's book *The Inconvenient Student: Critical Issues in the Identification and Education of Twice-Exceptional Students.*

○ **D**isabilities—a child's ability may not be realized if a disability prevents him or her from expressing talents, or if it affects achievement. A comprehensive evaluation can be useful in determining if a child has dual exceptionalities, learning issues, or vulnerabilities—and what kinds of accommodations to try.

○ **D**rawing/**D**rama/**D**ance/—some children have gifted-level abilities in art, or theatrical performance, or other areas that may not be addressed fully at their school. Parents have to be proactive in seeking ways to enable kids to develop and showcase their talents.

○ **D**esk—every student needs a place to think and work effectively—with adequate light, the necessary school supplies, and enough quiet to be able to concentrate. A nook in the attic—or under the stairs (like Harry Potter had)—is not ideal. But it's better than no place at all!

○ **D**elicate matters—sometimes children ask elusive or tricky questions about giftedness, ones that are poignant or that cause adults to stop and ponder… Questions like: "*Will I always be gifted? Why don't I feel smart? Is Grandma gifted? Are you? How do I know if I'm gifted?*") Think carefully before responding. Find out more when you don't know enough to answer children's questions. Consider finding out more together.

○ **D**iscussion—talk about these questions, and others that may arise, answering them honestly, while keeping in mind the child's age and level of understanding.

○ **D**emands—sometimes teachers give gifted learners too much work, piling on the demands, rather than providing more suitable (and reasonable) learning opportunities. Students may have to speak up— respectfully, of course, and preferably with a practical plan in mind.

Dispositions (directed toward taking action…)

○ **D**esire—it's not enough to be bright, it's important to *want* to learn.

○ **D**irection—all children need guidance and help to stay on course, and to navigate the daily do's and don'ts. Laura Markham has an information-laden website Aha! Parenting,[24] and she has written the *Peaceful Parent: Happy Kids* series of books. She provides advice in many areas including how parents can regulate themselves, and how to foster connection—and she shares strategies for emotion coaching, offering loving guidance, and supporting mastery, to help parents raise kids who are happy and also compassionate, self-disciplined, productive, and thoughtful.

○ **D**eliberation—thinking, planning, monitoring, and reflecting on outcomes—all of these are important to personal growth and achievement.

○ **D**reams—there's more to life than facts and figures! Where would we—or poets, or scientists, or athletes, or *anyone*—be without hopes and dreams?

○ **D**ispel misconceptions—there are lots of myths and mistaken beliefs connected with giftedness. We have to strengthen understandings of what giftedness is, and is not.

○ **D**iscipline—set boundaries that are fair and kind. Try setting them together. Even the smartest kids may have difficulty with behavior. This can be especially true if they become frustrated, bored, or have difficulty fitting in or coping with challenge or change. Be thoughtfully responsive when children act out (take a deep calming breath) but also look for ways to prevent behavioral problems from starting in the first place—and from escalating. Vanessa Lapointe writes about this in her book *Discipline without Damage: How to Get Your Kids to Behave without Messing Them Up*. She examines why children behave as they do, and what supports are needed in order to "*champion their healthy development.*" Ariadne Brill is an expert in "positive discipline" and, in the course of her work, she emphasizes the benefits of warm and patient communication, and helping children feel capable. She writes about how to raise children "*using mutual respect, trust, acceptance, and loving guidance*" in her book *Twelve Alternatives to Time Out: Connected Discipline*.

○ **D**ecision-making—choosing the right school, program, or learning options—*for* and *with* a child—takes time, information, thought, a collaborative approach, and diligence.

○ **D**oldrums—when children are not challenged sufficiently they can become bored or despondent. (The doldrums is a dull, drab, desolate place where nothing ever changes and nothing ever happens.) When learning drags due to dreariness or despair, perk things up! Discover creative alternatives, the unexpected, and rousing, imaginative, and stimulating choices.

○ **D**oubts—even the smartest people can experience misgivings about their abilities. Timely and targeted encouragement, and positive reinforcement, can dispel doubts.

○ **D**emonstrate—parents and teachers can model the kinds of dispositions and actions that will serve children well in different situations, including during troubling times, and when things go off kilter.

○ **D**umbo—a different kind of elephant, he was able to fly by flapping his ears. Now that's a gift! Triumph is often a matter of daring and perspective...

○ **D**are—why not??? Giftedness depends on learning, and learning requires effort and an enterprising spirit.

○ **D**estiny—no one is born smart. We each create our own destiny, and we become who we are based on how we assemble the many pieces of life's puzzles, over time.

○ **D**elight—share the happiness and pride you feel *about* your children *with* your children, and help create new and joyous destinies—day by day by day.

E is for Education

Every chapter of this book is like an **e**ntryway. I hope to **e**nergize readers, and **e**xpose them to current information, organized **e**fficiently.

There are many **E** words that relate meaningfully to giftedness and gifted **e**ducation at home, school, and beyond. Here I **e**xpand upon some **e**xplicit **e**xamples—with an **e**mphasis on: 1) the *essence of the exceptionality*, and 2) *external and experiential elements*.

I invite **e**veryone to:

1) *engage* with the material (considering how it might be useful to them);

2) *entertain* their own thoughts about each of the points;

3) *elaborate* upon the ideas; and thereby

4) *enhance* their understandings about gifted/high-level development.

The Essence of the Exceptionality

○ **E**xplanation—giftedness is exceptional ability in one or more areas, such that a learner requires educational adaptations.

○ **E**xceeding—gifted learners are those whose capabilities in some subjects markedly surpass those of their age or grade peers.

○ **E**xcellence—setting the bar high—but reasonably so—can inspire children, instilling a drive to strive that can culminate in excellence.

○ **E**ase—gifted learners do not necessarily find things easy; they often work vigorously to reach extended levels of understanding—which may be higher than that of their peers and require work.

○ **E**motional intelligence (also called emotional literacy)—helping children recognize and understand feelings enables them to be open-minded, empathic, and respectful of others.[25] Mary Gordon's book, *Roots of Empathy: Changing the World Child by Child* is a mesmerizing read about how to help children develop emotional intelligence, authentic communication with others, social strengths, and empathy. *The Roots of Empathy* program, for children 5 to 13, is being delivered in classrooms around the world.[26] It is "baby-driven," the strategies are scientifically grounded, and the focus is on dignity, compassion, acceptance, and social/emotional competence. Gordon writes about the importance of *"creating citizens of the world—children who are developing empathic ethics and a sense of responsibility...who will build a more caring, peaceful, and civil society, child by child."*

○ Empathy—success in life depends on being able to get along with people, and empathy is integral to that. However, it is not a trait that is inborn. Like intelligence, empathy must be cultivated from an early age. Many would argue that empathy is every bit as important as intelligence, if not more so, because it affects well-being, health, relationships, resilience, and future happiness. In *Unselfie: Why Empathetic Kids Succeed in Our All-About-Me World*, author Michele Borba discusses the unfortunate rise of self-absorption among children, and she provides insight into the essential competencies that comprise empathy. It's not enough to be smart. It imperative to be empathetic. Dr. Borba's parenting blog focuses on empathy, bullying prevention, and other character and social-emotional development issues.[27]

○ **E**minence—few gifted or extremely talented children ever achieve a high degree of eminence. Moreover, there are too many unknowns to be able to predict which children will become successful adults in a given domain, let alone who might achieve national, international, or public prominence. An interesting book is *Cradles of Eminence* by Victor Goertzel, Mildred Goertzel, Ted Goertzel, and Ariel Hansen. The authors discuss the childhoods of hundreds of famous individuals, describing their struggles, and the manner in which each ultimately attained success.

○ **E**nterprise and **E**ntrepreneurship—combine a sense of commitment with the longing to succeed, then build upon proficiencies, venture out on a limb, and voila! Kids can develop an entrepreneurial mind-set—that is, they can become invested in problem-solving, create value, learn about decision-making, develop some acumen or shrewdness in a domain of choice, and maybe even start their own business initiatives. To learn more about the importance of self-reliance and independence, and the possibilities of entrepreneurship, listen to the inspiring episodes at Tameka Montgomery's Raising Entrepreneurs Podcast.[28] Also, visit Julia Neiman's website and blog for skill-building tips for teens and young aspiring entrepreneurs.[29]

○ **E**xploration—learning is a multi-tiered investigative process, fueled by inspiration, anchored by determination, and enhanced by discovery—from infancy onward.

○ **E**thnicity—children should be proud of who they are, *and* who they are becoming. It's vital that adults continue to show why this is true. Our roots help to sustain us as we grow.

○ **E**xpertise—the term *"expert"* is typically reserved for adults. It applies to those who have attained exceedingly strong capabilities or have mastered certain skills, based on acquired know-how and practice, practice, practice.

○ **E**arned—*"Greatness is never a given. It must be earned."* (Stated by U.S. President Barack Obama during his inaugural address, Jan. 21, 2009.)

○ **E**ntitlement—as indicated by the quote above, kids have to harness responsibility and determination in order to build their gateways to achievement. Know-how and confidence are keys, whereas entitled attitudes and too much self-focus can be detrimental. Amy McCready's book *The Me, Me, Me Epidemic: A Step-By-Step Guide to Raising Capable, Grateful Kids in an Over-Entitled World* addresses issues having to do with entitlement, including strategies for *"creating a consequential environment"* and *"uncentering their universe."* Her Positive Parenting Solutions blog has articles relating to entitlement and other areas of concern.[30]

○ **E**thics—doing the right thing, having integrity, showing responsibility—these are examples of extra-cognitive factors that are integral to advanced development, academic and otherwise.

○ **E**xperiences—life is full of them, and they influence how we choose to use—or not use—our various inner and cultivated strengths.

External and Experiential Elements

○ **E**ncouragement—children benefit when they are given that extra boost, even in its simplest form such as a word, a nod, a smile, a thumbs-up, or a pat on the back.

○ **E**ngagement—not all advanced learners are enthusiastic, productive or motivated to achieve. Parents and teachers can motivate children and sustain their engagement in tasks by ensuring that learning is relevant, interesting, and appropriately challenging, and by offering support along the way.

○ **E**arly entrance to college or university—some teens are extremely academically advanced, and they graduate high school well before their age-peers. Others who have not yet graduated choose to participate in college-level courses to engage with more stimulating or challenging content. Those students who embark on post-secondary studies earlier than most are able to pursue specific areas of interest and strength in greater depth, and often with more sophistication than others their age. However, many parents worry about how their bright but comparatively young teen will adjust to the challenges of college life, especially when there are age discrepancies, social considerations, transitions, unfamiliar surroundings, and the many pressures that go along with being on a college or university campus—whether residing in a dorm or still living at home. In *Don't Go, Please Leave*, Sara Dimerman writes about possible concerns such as sleep deprivation, promiscuity, drinking, underachievement issues, increased independence, and the *"push/pull of emotions that parents and their teens experiences as dynamics shift between them and the family."* And, Johns Hopkins Center for

Talent Development has online information on early college entrance programs (primarily residential).[31]

○ **Effort**—never underestimate the importance of persistence and hard work; and never underestimate the value of reinforcing children's and teen's efforts. Artist Pablo Picasso said, "*I am always doing that which I cannot do in order that I may learn how to do it.*"

○ **Extracurricular** activities—help kids make the most of exciting, collaborative, and individually targeted learning opportunities beyond those that might be available during the regular school day.[32] Leadership roles, labs, competitions, internships, volunteerism, clubs—get creative! As I write elsewhere, "*Extracurricular activities provide an exploratory and social outlet for children, enabling them to extend their boundaries in venues that are often considerably less formal than traditional schooling… Ultimately, children should find pleasure in the supplementary activities in which they choose to participate, and they should be able to define a sense of accomplishment that is not based on grades.*"[33]

○ **Environment**—a learning environment can be any place where a person can discover something new. The most conducive setting (or, potentially, classroom) is one that is safe, enabling, comfortable, and challenging—in a good way.

○ **Enrichment**—encourage children to take advantage of the many programs expressly set up within schools and communities for the purpose of providing high-level and extended learning options in different areas of interest.

○ **Errors**—view them as stepping-stones to learning rather than roadblocks or obstacles, remembering to apply this to your own life, as well to your child's experiences.

○ **Exercise**—it is not enough to stimulate children's minds in the absence of other forms of stimulation. Physical activity is important for optimal health, and general well-being.

○ **Expectations**—think Goldilocks—not too high, not too low, but just right.

○ **E**conomic disadvantage—there are many school-based, community-oriented, government-funded, and philanthropic-generated programs that endeavor to give *all* children the chance to succeed, even when economic realities are harsh. When these programs partner with schools it can make a huge difference—setting new precedents, contributing ideas and financial support, and enabling stakeholders to connect with resources, engage in constructive dialogue, and create avenues for learning.

○ **E**litism—some people think that special education for gifted learners is a perk, and that tailored academic opportunities smack of elitism. But would these same charges hold true at the lower end of the learning spectrum? Each child is entitled to an education commensurate with his or her abilities, whatever those may be.

○ **E**quity—children should have their learning needs met regardless of ancestry, culture, race, gender identification, language, physical ability, religion, socio-economic status or any other factors related to personal identity. There must be a concerted effort to better identify and serve students from underserved and underrepresented groups. It's critical to detect and eliminate barriers and discriminatory practices that lead to inequitable outcomes, and that can have a negative impact on children's achievement and well-being. An education equity action plan provides a kind of blueprint toward equity, and it can be a helpful resource for deliberate and renewed focus. (Check this endnote link to see one such plan that has been developed for the province of Ontario, Canada.[34])

○ **E**valuation—teachers can choose from a broad array of fair and effective evaluation processes for students, including established methods, creative approaches, co-created and pre-set rubrics, and countless other options. Parents can advocate for resources for the pedagogical reference shelves in their child's school so teachers have reliable materials that they can readily consult, and that address evaluation, and other practices in gifted education.

○ **E**arly learning—very important! Play, in particular, is a fundamental way for children to learn, socialize, try things out, develop skill sets, and share. Play is enabling—in SO many ways. (Whereas too much time spent sitting and staring at screens is not.) Play outdoors is especially beneficial—cognitively, physically, creatively, emotionally, socially.... In the book *Balanced and Barefoot: How Unrestricted Outdoor Play Makes for Strong, Confident, and Capable Children*, author Angela Hanscom discusses the many benefits of outdoor play, including awakening the senses, fostering independence, promoting healthy motor development, and providing opportunities to be creative and to try out new activities. She writes, "*In nature, children learn to take risks, overcome fears, make new friends, regulate emotions, and create imaginary worlds.*" Author Gloria Van Donge also recognizes the value of play. Her *Cheetah Stories* can be read with young children. The colorful series helps little ones better understand gifted-related challenges and strengths, and the value of play alongside other learning experiences. And, in the book *Rest, Play, Grow: Making Sense of Preschoolers (Or Anyone Who Acts Like One)*, author Deborah MacNamara delves into developmental science in reader-friendly fashion—appreciating that young children "*illuminate the beginnings from which we grow*" and revealing "*what every young child wishes their adults understood about them.*" Her Kid's Best Bet blog"[35] has informative articles on various aspects of child development.

○ **Eligibility**—most school districts have policies that determine which students can or cannot participate in gifted programs, typically by virtue of attaining a certain cut-off score on an IQ test, or excelling at designated criteria. Happily, there is momentum toward more inclusive gifted identification practices that are flexibly responsive to a broader population of learners and their individual strengths, enabling a larger cadre of children to participate in gifted programming options.

○ **End**—no way! There are 21 letters to go!

F is for Fit and Flexibility

How can parents and teachers foster individual abilities, and facilitate foundational supports, so children will flourish? FYI—there's no fast or flawless formula. However, readers can use these **F** words to flesh out, fill in, fine-tune, or formulate a framework of factors they might want to think about or focus on in relation to supporting and encouraging children's gifted/high-level abilities.

The focus of this feature is 1) *fit* (between a student and learning opportunities), and 2) *flexibility* (on the part of all those involved in nurturing a child's development).

Fit: What Matters

Things go best for children when they have the opportunity to participate in learning and other activities that are well suited to their developmental levels, and readiness. These change over time, and therefore it can be challenging to find the right match between what a child can or will do at any point in time, and the sort of expectations that are laid forth. Moreover, this *fit* is not always obvious, simply tailored, or accessible. That's why parental support and guidance are so important, along with a willingness to be flexible—that is, to adapt to circumstances as they arise.

Flexibility: What Matters

It makes sense for parents to show consistency, and also to be firm when it benefits their child's welfare. For example, with respect to health, safety, or the family's well-being. There are times when it's absolutely necessary for parents to stand their ground. (Bike helmets, sunscreen, seat belts—some things are not up for negotiation.) However, there are also times when give and take, or compromise, are called for, and when the best response or approach involves being open to different ideas. Parents who are unyielding or controlling run the risk of missing opportunities to foster their children's autonomy, creativity, resilience, and confidence. Children need choice, and encouragement when they want to try new things. It helps when parents understand how children learn[36]—and recognize that each child is different. When parents show flexibility, children better appreciate the role of flexibility in their own lives.

Fit

○ **Fortitude**—spunk, a venturesome attitude, and the drive to forge ahead—all of which fuel the fire that sparks high-level ability.

○ **Future**—it's unknown. Like potential…

○ **Friendships**—relationship-building is not always easy. Children may need guidance when learning to navigate social landscapes like classrooms, playgrounds, and activity groups, in search of one or more friends with whom to share time, ideas, interests, activities, and fun. Eileen Kennedy-Moore's online site Dr. Friendtastic offers *"friendship advice for kids,"* and information for parents and teachers.[37]

○ **Formal identification**—the traditional approach of identifying, labeling, and then segregating children on the basis of general intelligence or academic test scores (usually based on performance at a single point in time), is very hard to defend. A child's learning needs are better determined by means of multiple measures, including ongoing assessment that is individually responsive, integrated into instruction, and subject-specific. (That said, standardized tests *can* be useful for providing additional information and objective confirmation of teacher judgment and other assessment data.)

○ **Flow**—a state of being wherein one is totally immersed in an engaging task—like a perfect fit between person and project—such that realities like time or fatigue, or daily distractions seem to fade away, and a sense of satisfaction prevails.

○ **Foresight**—taking a thoughtful, discretionary approach will likely lead to sensible decision-making. For example, about educational choices or program options or advocacy.

○ **Fairness**—gifted learners don't need or want more work. They need and want *meaningful, appropriately challenging* activities. Encourage children's involvement in planning learning experiences, and in setting reasonable standards for which they can then be held accountable.

○ **Fulfillment**—that fine feeling when the learner-learning fit is fruitful.

○ **Feedback**—timely, appropriate, constructive, and honest feedback stimulates further inquiry, and motivates children to progress to the next level in their learning.

○ **Falling short?**—countless excellent teachers offer wonderful learning experiences differentiating programs, challenging students, and empowering them to become life-long learners. (Fabulous!) However, imagine how fantastic it would be if even more teachers tapped into professional development opportunities in gifted education, and adopted programming methods designed to facilitate high-level learning for *all* pupils.

○ **Fast-tracking**—a term that implies moving ahead at a pace that is quicker and presumably better suited to high-ability learners. This may take different forms such as advanced programming, acceleration, or more sophisticated curriculum content.

○ **Findings**—research continues to enlighten as to how children learn, and what parents and teachers can do. There are many scholarly journals that can be found online, and on shelves in reference libraries. For example, the National Association for Gifted Children publishes the journal *Gifted Child Quarterly* which provides interesting articles about studies in the field of giftedness and gifted education.[38]

○ **Followers**—there are two types of people—those who lead and those who follow. Be a leader. Or follow someone or something meaningful and good.

Flexibility

○ **F**orces of nature—there are many things we cannot control in life. We have to learn to accept what is feasible, fix what is flawed, and live flexibly. And teach children to do likewise.

○ **F**ailure—fizzle, funk, fiasco, flop, faults, fumbles, folly—any of which can frustrate—or lead to growth and further learning. Whoever said success was foolproof? Learning is about making mistakes. *The Gift of Failure: How the Best Parents Learn to Let Go So Their Children Can Succeed* is a carefully researched and beautifully written book by Jessica Lahey. It's a welcome addition to the literature on children's resilience, independence, and competence. And Michael Michalko has written an article on successful people who overcame failure and rose to the top of their respective fields.[39]

○ **F**amily dynamics—a supportive family is formative—advising, enriching, encouraging, and caring. Brandie Weikle shares articles and over 200 podcasts that reflect modern views of family life on her New Family website.[40] Also Alyson Schafer's three books—*Ain't Misbehaving*, and *Honey, I Wrecked the Kids*, and *Breaking the Good Mom Myth*—are full of tips, but with a humorous touch. And, Wendy **S**kinner reveals her family's experiential struggles and successes in her book, *Life with Gifted Children.*

○ **F**amily meetings—regular family meetings provide opportunities for family members to connect and stay on track with one another. These times can be enjoyable, enhance communications, help organize everyone's comings and goings, and be a catalyst for sharing and appreciating one another's plans and activities. See the endnotes for a resource with more information about family meetings.[41]

○ **F**unding—educational systems require funding to function. However, exciting learning options don't have to cost a fortune. There are recreation and community centres, libraries, museums, galleries, and outdoor venues. Foundations also raise funds for educational opportunities, youth groups, and organizations that offer various kinds of learning experiences.

○ **F**ixed mindset—the inflexible and unfortunate belief that giftedness is fixed or innate (no, it's not), and that abilities cannot be furthered with learning provisions and effort (yes, they can!).

○ **F**eats—accomplishments come in different formats, fabrications, and fashions. Achievements don't have to be flashy or foremost to be first-rate... And, flaunting and flair are not necessarily fortuitous.

○ **F**eelings—they frequently fluctuate—and parents have to stay attuned to the various factors and influences that affect children's emotional functioning. Adults can read Stuart Shanker's book *Self-Reg* for practical skill-building suggestions for kids.

○ **F**un—learning can be fun, challenging, and inspiring. In fact, fun is just the beginning.

○ **F**aculties of education—where teachers learn the fundamentals of teaching, and ideally, there are fully-attended course offerings in gifted education! Alas, these are too few, and far between...

○ **F**ast workers—not all high-ability learners fly through tasks. A fastidious approach—slow, steady, thoughtful, and purposeful—can be better than flurrying.

○ **F**act and **F**iction—understandings of giftedness run the gamut between what's true and what's false; what's fine and what's feared; what's real and what's presumed. It's important to be accurately and well-informed about gifted-related issues.

○ **F**uss—don't fret about children's giftedness. Embrace it, have faith in their ability, and let it be fulfilling!

○ **F**ate—chance, luck, fortune, destiny... These are unfathomable unknowns that accompany hard work and favorable opportunities, and that can lead to future success and well-being.

G is for Gifted

> Giftedness can generate speculation, misconceptions, expectations, pride, innuendo, apprehension, puzzlement, and on and on and on…
>
> In this chapter, I grapple with the term *"gifted,"* and give a glimpse into 1) the *gist of giftedness*, along with 2) *general guidelines* for children's optimal growth, whether one is formally identified as a gifted learner, or not. I hope readers think about these **G** words, and use them to engender greater understanding.

Gifted: What Matters

A child's current achievements are works in the making, and future accomplishments are unknown. Cultivating gifted-level development is a multi-faceted endeavor. A person has to be effortful—willing and able to practice skills and to persevere; resilient—open to seeing setbacks as growth opportunities; and passionate—keen to extend capabilities and knowledge in those areas in which they choose to excel.

Ongoing research in child development, educational psychology, neurological science, and related fields continues to inform parents, teachers, health professionals, and others about giftedness, including how children learn, how educators should teach, and how parents can support their children at home and school. This involves how to better identify and address learning issues: how to acquire information on strategies for responsive teaching and parenting; how to develop curriculum and learning experiences; and how to engage in collaborative practices that send positive messages and strengthen home, school, and community connections.

Moreover, recent studies have shown that giftedness is not just about intellectual ability, or *"head strengths."* A child's happiness, well-being, and success are also dependent upon the development of *"heart strengths."* (See the article "Lessons Learned from Working with High-Ability Students" by psychologist Stephen Pfeiffer.[42]) These heart strengths include humility, respect for others, compassion, enthusiasm, kindness, and integrity. We need more school-based programs that value, teach, and reinforce important virtues like these, in addition to the standard academic subjects—from preschool all the way through college. These personal strengths cannot actually grow stronger unless they are given proper emphasis and are addressed by parents, teachers, mentors, extended family, and others who are pivotal in children's lives.

Talent development provides a framework for giftedness. Identifying and addressing children's abilities across different domains means that educators not only focus on high cognitive capabilities (as might transpire when a gifted classification occurs on the basis of a high IQ score) but that gifted education is attentive to other specific areas of strength. For example, this might include art, drama, music, sports, or science. Education should nurture children's talents regardless of where they might lie, and identification and programming practices should be reflective of this. In *Talent Development as a Framework for Gifted Education: Implications for Best Practices and Applications in Schools* (edited by Paula Olszewski-Kubilius, Rena Subotnik, and Frank C. Worrell), many experts in gifted education come together to present views across a range of themes. Although this book is written primarily for educators, it provides comprehensive guideline for parents who want more information about talent development and giftedness.

There are also education centers all around the world that are dedicated to identifying and developing children's gifted-level abilities. One such noted facility is Johns Hopkins Center for Talented Youth.[43] CTY focuses on research, advocacy, and counselling services, and offers a broad array of online, international, and summer, and family-oriented programs. CTY also provides information on above grade-level testing, diagnostics, early college entrance programs, internships, and research opportunities.

Supportive adults are an important factor in whether or not children will succeed to the utmost of their ability. Here are some ideas to help parents who are grappling with understandings about giftedness, and who are wondering how to maximize their children's abilities.

Giftedness: The Gist of the G Word

○ **G**iftedness—"*Intelligence is neither innate nor fixed. It's not an attribute owned exclusively by some people, and not by others. The pathways to exceptional achievement are complex, diverse, and socially constructed, varying across individuals, developmental periods, contexts and cultures. Intelligence and, perhaps just as importantly, creativity, develop over time, and can be influenced by many factors.*" (Extracted from *Beyond Intelligence: Secrets for Raising Happily Productive Kids* by Dona Matthews and Joanne Foster, pp. 239-240.)

○ **G**ifted education—the most suitable learning opportunities are those that meet children's individual and diverse learning needs; and provisions will vary from one individual to the next on a situational and subject-by-subject basis. It is incumbent upon teachers of gifted learners to consolidate and build upon their understandings of giftedness and related issues, and to develop the strategies and competencies they require in order to create effective programs, address children's needs, and encourage lifelong learning. To that end, teacher training and professional development should focus on the honing of educators' pedagogical skills, and on appropriate practices for teaching gifted/high-ability learners. (Parents can advocate for this!)

○ **G**enius—someone who has demonstrated exceptional achievement in an important field, such as Leonardo Da Vinci, Stephen Hawking, Shakespeare, Beethoven, and Galileo.

○ **G**uarantees—no one knows what the future holds, so there is no sure-fire way to ascertain who is likely to succeed. However, effort and persistence are germane.

○ **G**aps—gifted learners can have gaps or glitches or even gaping holes in their knowledge or skill sets and, like others, may require assistance to grasp concepts—and get to the next level of learning.

○ **G**lobally gifted—few people have exceptional or gifted-level ability across all domains. Savvy educators adapt instruction in order to meet individuals' particular needs.

○ "**G**eek"—there are times in a child's life when being "cool"—or conversely, being a "nerd"—can make all the difference between fitting in or being left out, doing well or doing poorly, feeling glad or feeling gloomy. Self-image can be fragile and complex. Children who experience periods of social or emotional vulnerability may need extra support from parents, teachers, or others in order to stay grounded. A helpful resource is *On the Social and Emotional Lives of Gifted Children, 5th Edition* by Tracy Cross.

○ **G**rown-ups—children count on grown-ups for help in getting through the ups and downs of daily life. Don't take this responsibility for granted. Be there.

○ **G**atekeepers—the adults in children's lives are conduits for their learning. Be careful not to impede or otherwise block gateways for development. Safeguard children's comings and goings. Provide direction and keep communication channels open.

Giftedness: General Guidelines for Growth

○ **G**enuine—feedback and encouragement should be sincere. Make it real. Make it matter. Make it often.

○ **G**o!—propulsion/forward motion. Gratifying, gainful, and there's nothing else like it...

○ **G**enerosity of spirit—the most brilliant mind is bankrupt if the moral and ethical coffers are bare. Teach children to be good people, to contribute to society, and to be gracious.

○ Curious **G**eorge—the protagonist of a series of children's books, George is an outgoing, inquisitive monkey (created by Hans Augusto Rey and Margret Rey). He adapts to the big city, has many exciting adventures, and learns a great deal because he is so gregarious.

○ **G**randparents—so much love to give, and so many "grand" times to share. Make the most of every generational-bridging minute! Consider having a look at *Grandparents' Guide to Gifted Children* by James Webb,

Janet Gore, Frances Karnes, and Stephen McDaniel. The authors discuss the unique role that grandparents can play in nurturing children's gifted-level abilities.

○ **G**alleries—there are many different kinds of go-to venues where children can learn more about the world, and all its grandeur.

○ **G**alvanize—regardless of how old you are, it helps to have a place to gravitate for inspiration, relaxation, strength, solace, and opportunities to think, write, or create. A corner, a cozy chair, a park, a playground, a certain neighbourhood, or some other locale. I happen to like Gravenhurst, a small Canadian lake-side town where the sun sparkles on the water, the air is fresh, the rock formations are stunning, and I can unwind and feel revitalized.

○ **G**roups—some children function well in groups, others prefer to work independently, or perhaps more guardedly. Group activities should be opportunities for children to share ideas, and to feel valued. Variables to consider include size, individual learning modes, ability levels, compatibility, attitudinal factors, and motivation.

○ **G**irls—vastly improved gender equity policies and practices are helping to ensure that more girls are motivated, make sound school choices, and achieve to the best of their ability. Support them in exploring their interests and capabilities early on, through adolescence, and beyond. In the book *Smart Girls in the 21st Century: Understanding Talented Girls and Women,* Barbara Kerr and Robyn McKay offer an abundance of information about giftedness, barriers, educational issues, self-actualization, and a wide range of important considerations relating to smart girls. And, *No More Mean Girls: The Secret to Raising Strong, Confident, and Compassionate Girls* by Katie Hurley is a must-read read for parents, teachers, and caregivers.

○ **G**oogle—one of countless search engines designed to enable people to engage in research, and extend their boundaries of inquiry and learning, all around the globe.

○ **G**ames—high-level development starts with playful exploration, proceeding through skill acquisition, and then increasing mastery. Play can motivate, stimulate thought processes, and enhance children's social, emotional, and cognitive abilities. Game-playing enables kids to learn about reciprocal interactions, to build skill sets, and to manage a range of feelings under conditions that are (hopefully) safe and enjoyable.

○ **G**uidance—gentle but firm. Offer and provide it if or when needed. Honor children's questions and concerns. Children benefit from connectivity that is attuned to their particular needs, and that is supportive of their particular challenges. Kids learn from what we do, not only from what we say. A gentle, thoughtful, respectful, and compassionate approach can help to soothe anger, worries, doubt, disappointment, and other feelings that kids inevitably experience.

○ **G**oal-setting—help children learn to set reasonable objectives, ones that are realistic, timely, and affirming, and encourage them to strive to reach their goals. For information on goal-setting, see *Peak Performance for Smart Kids: Strategies and Tips for School Success* by Maureen Neihart, and also my book *Bust Your BUTS: Tips for Teens Who Procrastinate*.

○ **G**umption—the courage to be yourself. The will to move ahead. The strength of character and mind that brings about progress. All of which show grit, and which can gradually lead to greatness.

H is for Health and Happiness

As you read these **H** words, think about what you can do to encourage kids to be **h**ealth-conscious, and to feel good about their daily experiences and themselves. Their **health** and **happiness** will have an impact on **h**ow they learn and grow.

Health and Happiness: What Matters

What do parents want most for their children? No two families are exactly the same, so one might surmise a broad range of responses to that question. However, two ideals immediately come to mind: to keep children healthy and happy.

Neither outcome is automatic. Health has to be nurtured, and respected. Children, especially, have to be safeguarded because their daily and long-term prospects for good health are dependent upon the care they are given. Happiness, too, is contingent upon many factors, regardless of age. Babies, toddlers, tweens, adolescents—they all experience relationships, challenges, disappointments, uncertainties, and lots of different emotions. Happiness is just one of these, and it can also be elusive.

The ways in which parents help children generate positive outcomes differ from one family to the next. There is no one script or set framework that will shield kids from all the difficulties in life, or that will guarantee that they'll grow up being happy and healthy. However, there are some constructive starting points that all parents can reflect upon, and they follow here.

Harnessing Health

○ **H**urrying—we live in a complex and ever-changing world. People tend to scurry, and often struggle to keep pace. Sometimes we have to learn to decelerate a bit, and teach kids to do the same, also showing them how to be resilient if, in haste, they stumble along the way.[44]

○ **H**olistic—so many body parts all working in sync! However, when one part goes out of whack things can go awry. Help children understand the importance of keeping their bodies tuned. This includes organs, limbs, muscles, and so on—as well as the mind (awareness, spirit, emotions, and intellect).

○ **H**eart—our brains make us unique, but the heart's pumping is at the core of what keeps us going. Hearty and nourishing foods provide the nutrients for a strong circulatory system, which in turn generates power to exercise thought, and take action. Children can be taught to make the right kinds of healthy food choices throughout the day so that they feel energized and ready to learn.

○ **H**abits of mind—effort, perseverance, and practice open up possibilities for heightened development, and a healthy mindset for learning. If you haven't seen the book *The Seven Habits of Highly Effective Teens* by Sean Covey you may want to have a look. By way of encapsulating, the first three habits are to be proactive, start with the end in mind, and put first things first. The next four habits are to think win/win, seek first to understand and then be understood, synergize, and finally to engage in renewal and continual improvement. Each of these habits is explained fully by the author.

○ **H**elp—people often need support and guidance to persevere or to make good decisions. Sometimes we need less help, and sometimes we need more. Help may be academic, medical, physical, spiritual, or some other form altogether. Smart people are not afraid to ask for assistance. They know that getting help can ease the way, and also help to make them smarter and stronger.

○ **H**ercules—this mythological hero far surpassed all mere mortals in strength, size, and skill. He lost (and later regained) his sanity. Even the strongest characters are not always hale and hearty, and they may have issues or experiences that tax their well-being. Teach children to be accepting of the disparities and fluctuations in their abilities, and also to be considerate of others. Suitably targeted mythical stories can jumpstart conversations about courage and compassion.

○ **H**onesty—it's best if children have someone they trust and with whom they can talk about their ups and downs, concerns, relationships, schooling, and every-day lives. Bottling things up is not healthy.

○ **H**eed—red flags include lack of sleep, disordered eating, suspected drug or alcohol use, being unkempt, hyperactivity, depression, loneliness, rage, abusive behavior—and if there is concern, then it's wise to call in a professional to help deal with the issues. For example, this might be a pediatrician or medical practitioner, a school counselor, a clinical psychologist, a social worker, or other supports. A family doctor should be able to offer suggestions.

○ **H**ollingworth—back in the 1920s, Leta Hollingworth made significant contributions to the field of education by focusing on the guidance and counseling needs of gifted learners. Her work is still highly regarded today. Her story comes to life in the book *A Forgotten Voice,* wherein author Anne Klein describes Hollingworth's considerable impact on gifted education, feminism, and psychology.

Harnessing Happiness

○ **H**a-ha-ha—laughter is a means to communicate and share joy with others. It's an outlet for emotions, and a way to cope with stressful situations. It can empower, enliven, and even change the mood of an entire room. Laughter is a funny thing…

○ **H**ardwired—happiness is a state of being, and also a state of mind. The brain is like a control center for feelings, thoughts, actions, and communication. Neuropsychologist Rick Hanson writes that, *"the inner strengths we need for well-being, coping, and success are built from brain structure."* These strengths—including contentment, peacefulness, love, insight, and resilience—develop over time. Hanson explains how people can increase levels of happiness (*"hardwiring it"*) by *"taking in the good"* and transforming positive experiences to lasting improvements in "*neural net worth.*" In the book *Hardwiring Happiness: The New Brain Science of Contentment, Calm and Confidence,*" he describes how having, enriching, absorbing, and linking these experiences (HEAL) can lead to less vulnerability and negativity, and more mindfulness and joy.

○ **H**igh-level ability—something to be proud of! This entire ABCs book is about ways to raise kids to be smart—and resilient, compassionate, curious, joyful, flexible, productive, kind… And to embrace their strengths, and use them wisely and in ways that will benefit others.

○ **H**ope—Actor Christopher Reeve (aka Superman) stated these words: "*Once you choose hope, anything's possible.*" He sustained a spinal cord injury, and he became a quadriplegic. His strong message provides inspiration to anyone who may feel despair or disillusionment, who is struggling in some way, or who might need help to develop a positive outlook. For more on how to nurture hope and idealism so children can cope with difficulties, and acquire renewed perspectives, see *Searching for Meaning: Idealism, Bright Minds, Disillusionment, and Hope* by James Webb.

○ **H**ome—a safe haven; a place where children can relax, feel contentment, and connect with family members. And family values! In *How to be a Happier Parent: Raising a Family, Having a Life, and Loving (Almost) Every Minute,* K.J. Dell'Antonia writes about how to create a happy and satisfying family dynamic, and she includes plenty of strategies for "*taking it one trouble spot at a time.*"

○ **H**omeschooling—many parents choose to homeschool their children for a variety of reasons. These include more flexibility in teaching: a curriculum that is specifically and individually tailored; pacing opportunities that allow for a nuanced and easily adapted balance between learning and playing; and greater one-on-one connectivity. For more information on homeschooling, talk to parents who have chosen this option, and perhaps to their kids, too. And, explore online forums, resources, and interactive experiences such as those offered by Athena's Advanced Academy and other options posted on the Hoagies' website.[45]

○ **H**o **H**um—when children are bored, they are not motivated to learn. (Although they may be motivated to find out what they *want* to learn.)

○ **H**arangue and **H**over—when kids are berated, pestered, scrutinized, or helicoptered-over, they are not motivated to learn.

○ **H**ard—when the task is too difficult, they are not motivated to learn.

○ **H**assles—when an activity is problematic, they are not motivated to learn.

○ **H**eavy—when the workload is overwhelming, they are not motivated to learn.

○ a**H**a!—however, when children are appropriately challenged, they are likely to be happily productive!

○ **H**onor—respect children's choices, preferences, decisions, interests, and capabilities. Singer, song-writer, and child advocate, Raffi Cavoukian recently launched his vision and organization, Child Honouring. There is information online about how to "*regard and treat our young as the key to building a humane and sustainable world…*" including "*building community, restoring planetary health, peacemaking, and creating sustainable economies that support the well-being of children and families.*"[46]

○ **H**omework—it may seem odd to find this word beneath the "Harnessing Happiness" heading, however, *quality* homework can be gratifying. When homework assignments are relevant—that is, meaningful, not drill-and-kill, suitable in terms of difficulty, and respectful of time expectations—then they can serve to support students' learning goals. Granted, homework is a controversial topic, and not everyone welcomes what is sometimes perceived as superfluous or extra work. But through *appropriate* homework, kids can extend their knowledge, further analyze concepts, practice skills, and learn new ones. And, if the homework is fun, so much the better!

○ **H**armony—help children learn the value of teamwork, a collaborative spirit, and a sense of community, and to appreciate the satisfaction and enjoyment that can be had by co-creating with others.

○ **H**umor—knowing when and how to use humor is another way of being smart. Sometimes people use humor to mask pain or troubles (like the clown who is laughing on the outside but crying on the inside), and sometimes they use humor because they are bored and want something to happen (like the class clown). And, sometimes, they use humor inappropriately to hurt other people's feelings (like mockers or ridiculers). However, humor can also be a fine remedy for difficult moments or maladies. The type of humor that feels the best for kids is when they look on the bright side of things and laugh along with friends and family. Mark Twain said, *"Humor is mankind's greatest blessing."*

○ **H**obbies—pleasant pastimes, interesting learning opportunities, creative craftsmanship, or intricate handiwork... Maybe it's knitting, or sculpting, or star gazing, or chess, or magic tricks, or photography... Whatever children choose to pursue can start a lifelong passion!

○ **H**arvard—this well-known university in Cambridge, Massachusetts accepts only the very top echelon of high-achieving students, based on test scores and other specific criteria that attest to intellectual prowess. Some parents dream that one day their children will go to an educational institution like this. But remember, the important thing is not how hard a school is to get into, but rather how good the fit is between the student and the school. And, while on the topic of Harvard, their Center for the Developing Child provides interesting science-based and international resources on a range of topics including brain architecture, mental health, resilience, and more.[47]

○ **H**istory—the past informs the future. Historical accounts of happenings and humanity are like footprints to follow—or not—when navigating what lies ahead. Encourage children to read about historical figures, to think about their varied experiences, and to consider what can be learned from them.

○ **H**ooray!—give children positive reinforcement and acknowledge their efforts. Help them to feel good about their individual attributes. In *The Happy Kid Handbook: How to Raise Joyful Children in a Stressful World*, author Katie Hurley explains that when it comes to parenting, having an ideal blueprint of how things *should* go (including setting rules and expectations, having good intentions, and hoping for the best), just won't suffice. She begins with the concept *"know thy child,"* counsels that *"raising happy kids means striking the right balance for each child in the family,"* and explains how to *"parent the individual."* Hurley also has a Practical Parenting blog.[48]

○ **H**ugs—and cuddles and a smile convey more than words alone. There are other benefits, too. Comforting hugs can help to reduce stress, fear, and pain, and a supportive hug is a means of demonstrating support which can, in turn, promote happiness and even health. The children's book *Hugs,* written by Robert Munsch and illustrated by Michael Martchenko, is about getting and giving hugs—and reveals the best kind of all.

I Is for Independence and Initiative

In this installment, I implore parents to take the word "I" off the table. Instead of thinking *"What can I do for my children?"* consider, *"What can they learn to do for themselves?"* In other words, how can you invoke children's independence, and initiative? Start by inspiring them to investigate, imagine, and use their intellect. Here are some more ideas, which I introduce by formatting each distinctly as an ***inquiry*** (**?**) followed by an ***immediate idea*** (**→**) so as to provide impetus for implementation.

○ **I**dentify—What are your children's interests and learning goals?

→ **I**mmediate **I**dea—Encourage them to articulate these. Ask questions, without being too pushy. Chat about how to go about exploring possibilities.

○ **I**ncorporate—How might your children incorporate those interests and goals into what's happening at school?

→ **I**mmediate **I**dea—Start by co-creating just one or two action steps—perhaps to embark upon together at first—and then on their own, and let momentum build from there.

○ **I**mportant—What is most important to you when it comes to your children's education and well-being?

→ **I**mmediate **I**dea—And, what is most important to them? Think about how these objectives are aligned. Or can be better aligned.

○ **I**ntelligence edge—How can children develop the edge they will inevitably need—including learning to meet challenges, overcome obstacles, and manage change?

→ **I**mmediate **I**dea—These are acquired skills. Kids' lives are often whirlwinds of activity—punctuated by pressure to succeed. Adults' lives are like that, too. Consider slowing things down in order to create enough time for what really matters, such as dealing with issues that arise, leisure, play, and spending quality time together. Be sure to respect and discuss children's concerns, and model how to deal with them successfully.

○ **?** **I**ntegrity—Did this word come to mind in relation to the earlier question about what's important?

→ **I**mmediate **I**dea—Along with honesty, determination, responsibility, and other virtues, integrity builds character and fortifies children's moral fiber so they will act ethically as they forge ahead. Have a look at Marilyn Price-Mitchell's "Compass Advantage" framework depicting eight essential character strengths—including integrity—and how to nurture these.[49]

○ **?** **I**nformation—What kinds of resource access do you engage in to stay up-to-date on matters having to do with gifted/high-level development?

→ **I**mmediate **I**dea—When parents and teachers are well-informed, they are better positioned to encourage gifted-level outcomes in children. Information-gathering should be an ongoing process over the course of parenting and teaching, and should occur when things are running smoothly as well as when they are not because life never stays the same. Be informed and prepared. The pendulum is always swinging.

○ **?** **I**nsightful—How carefully do you listen to your children when they talk about their day?

→ **I**mmediate **I**dea—Children's perspectives are often far more insightful than we give them credit for. By getting a true understanding of children's daily experiences, we can reinforce their efforts and resilience, so they will progress to the next step—all the while knowing they have the support they need if things get too complicated or intense.

○ **?** **I**nterpret—How much do you know about assessment procedures?

→ **Immediate Idea**—Think about whether there are reports you'd like to have clarified or diagnostic procedures you want to find out more about, in order to be well-equipped to encourage your children to engage in suitable tasks, feel confident, and succeed.

○ **?** **I**nvest—In what ways are you invested in your children's education?

→ **Immediate Idea**—Not just monetary investment, but think in terms of daily interactions, ongoing communication channels, homework, technological know-how, social networking, and so on.

○ **?** **I**nvite—To what extent do you feel welcome in the school?

→ **Immediate Idea**—If you feel comfortable, you may want to become more involved in the school community. If not, think about speaking to the teacher about how to bridge the gap, without being intrusive. By increasing your involvement in the life of the school you become more attuned to the ebb and flow of learning processes, including how your kids learn best.

○ **?** **I**dentity—How well do you know what makes your children tick?

→ **Immediate Idea**—Throughout childhood and adolescence, the sense of self is a work in progress. Kids' responses, abilities, emotions, and identities are in flux. Some days are better than others. And so it is for everyone. Intelligent parenting involves knowing when to leave things be—or when to encourage, intervene, discipline, guide, or offer constructive advice or assistance—as children grow, stumble, succeed, and develop.

○ **?** **I**ssues—What kinds of concerns do you have, and what is being done to address them?

→ **Immediate Idea**—If a child is experiencing social, emotional, behavioral, motivational or academic problems, then it may be time for serious discussions with professionals who can provide some assistance.

For example, a guidance counselor, pediatrician, educational or clinical psychologist, or others who possess certain skills and expertise, may be able to help.

○ **? I**nclusion—Do your children feel "a part of" things or "apart from" things?

→ **Immediate Idea**—There's a big difference. Belonging is important. Whereas feeling disconnected, marginalized, different, separated, or categorized can make or break a child's school experience—depending on whether or not solid supports are in place. Individualism is good. Isolation is not.

○ **? I**nfluences—What influences affect your children's learning, at home and at school?

→ **Immediate Idea**—Family members? Friends? Extracurricular opportunities? Peer groups? Teachers? Cultural experiences? Books? Social media? Mentors? This is a short-list of possibilities. There are likely more. Plus, there are internal influences such as feelings, aspirations, and motivations. Be aware of the various influences and their possible impact, and be ready to help children be mindful and stay in control.

○ **? I**gnite—What sparks a child's imagination and intellectual growth?

→ **Immediate Idea**—Endless options! There's choice. Encouragement. Guidance. Self-confidence. Lots of opportunities to think, communicate, explore, and create. And letting children's fire or passion come from within. Step away from the blaze—but from time to time celebrate the sizzle, and help fan the flames…

○ **? I**nquisitiveness—Questions, both big and small, are a foundation of learning. Who asks and who answers in your house?

→ **Immediate Idea**—*"There is no such thing as a stupid question."* With that adage in mind, embrace inquiry-based learning, model and stimulate curiosity, and appreciate children's sense of wonder—all of which can lead to enhanced creativity and accomplishment.

○ **?** **I**mpossibilities—Sure, there are things that may seem out of reach... But, who can you think of, and what can you do, to help your family reach higher and stretch further?

→ Immediate **I**dea—We may not be able to catch a star, count all the seashells, or climb a mountain but there's lots we *can* do if only we try—and believe in ourselves. Lewis Carroll wrote, "*Sometimes I've believed in as many as six impossible things before breakfast.*" It's fun, and also potentially productive, to ponder possibilities...

○ **?** **I**deal—If you could make three wishes for each of your children, what would they be? Be practical...

→ **I**mmediate **I**dea—Realistically, how can you work together to make them come true?

J is for Journey

The saying, *"life is a journey"* may sound clichéd, but the words are nevertheless true. A journey is experienced step-by-step-by-step, one day (or juncture) at a time. Our personal journeys contribute to—and also define—who we are, and what we do in life. Abilities, and all the things we know, are like a passport to new and wondrous places we encounter.

Encourage children to find the joy in learning, wherever and whenever they can, by way of jaunts, jokes, jobs, jams, and jolly good times. Kids can also learn a great deal from the travels, directions, and adventures chosen by others, and especially from people whose life stories or experiences offer inspiration by virtue of their effort, perseverance, and acquired success.

What follows is a list of accomplished individuals whose last names all start with the letter **J**. They're representative of many men and women who have joined the top ranks in their fields by working hard, and jarring the status quo by juggling, jostling, or overcoming jeopardy. (It can be a jungle out there!) And, often their journeys are jubilant and just.

○ **All that Jazz**

Musicians enhance the landscape of musical performance through melodies, production, lyrics, or creative forays into song and dance. The people below carefully prepared, rehearsed, fine-tuned, and shared their craft—entertaining and enriching countless lives with music and talent.

Quincy **Jones** (trumpeter/composer/bandleader/producer); Mick **Jagger** (rock star); Janis **Joplin** (singer/songwriter); Billy **Joel** (pianist/singer/composer); Scott **Joplin** (ragtime composer/pianist); Elton **John** (singer/

songwriter/producer); Al **Jolson** (singer); **Jay-Z** (rapper/songwriter/record producer); Etta **James** (singer); Norah **Jones** (singer/songwriter)

○ Jockeying for Position

Exceptional athleticism involves practice, commitment, and a willingness to propel oneself toward excellence even when the competition is daunting. The athletes whose names appear here harnessed their strength, energy, and desire, and beat the odds to become exceptionally skilled in their respective sports. Being "gifted" or "talented" does not mean being confined to a desk, a library, or academic pursuits. There is much to be learned from sports-related activities. Babe Ruth said, *"Every strike brings me closer to the next home run."*

LeBron **James** (basketball); Michael **Jordan** (basketball); Bobby **Jones** (golf/founder of the Masters Tournament); Jackie **Joyner-Kersee** (multiple Olympic gold medalist, heptathlon); Reggie **Jackson** (baseball); Magic **Johnson** (basketball); Florence Griffith **Joyner** (multiple Olympic gold medalist, sprinting)

○ Joys of Jurisprudence (and political pursuit)

Public service and leadership are commendable, but not everyone has the inclination to work in the limelight, or the sustainability to succeed in the public sector. Those who make their mark and strive to improve the state of societal affairs often have interesting life stories, and it can be intriguing to see how tenacity, decisions, learning, and proficiencies can lead to triumph, and even have broad impact.

Andrew **Jackson** (7th US president, 1829-37); Jacob K. **Javits** (politician—many Javits Scholarships are awarded annually in support of students who exhibit excellence); John **Jay** (first Chief Justice of the US Supreme Court); Ruth Bader Ginsburg. (Although there's no **J** in her last name, she is a US Supreme Court **J**ustice, and is included here as representative of all women who engage in judiciary work.)

○ Jolting!

Talk about impact! Two techno-wizards revolutionized how we learn and acquire information, transforming the tools we use to express ourselves, and influencing the ways in which we communicate with others on a personal and a global scale. They spearheaded many technological break-throughs, and changed the history of how people use computers.

Steven **Jobs** (Founder of Apple Computers); Bill **Joy** (computer engineer who developed operating systems and software programs)

○ Jottings

Authors of all ages compose poems, articles, books, presentations, plays, and various other kinds of writing. Words can be extremely influential, and they have the power to change the way people think and act. Parents and teachers can encourage children to write and also to read; to find enlightening material, including audio books and podcasts; to share literary experiences; to record their reflective journeys in journals; and to reflect upon and discuss the different kinds of messages that words convey. The end result? Children develop meaningful understandings and learn to be discerning. Here are some wordsmiths.

James **Joyce** (*Ulysses*); James **Jones** (*From Here to Eternity*); P.D. **James** (author of many crime fiction and mystery novels); Thomas **Jefferson** (3rd US President, 1801-09, wrote first draft of *The Declaration of Independence*); Norton **Juster** (*The Phantom Tollbooth*—my favorite book!)

○ Creative Juices

Innovative thinkers have the capacity to alter lives, including how people look at the world, and how they engage with all it has to offer—perspectives, appreciation of the arts, personal attire, health, and so on. For example, the individuals mentioned below have influenced these aspects of everyday life, and how we enjoy or even extend them. Who has transformed the way *you* live? And what lies beneath, and beyond?

Marc **Jacobs** (fashion designer); Carl **Jung** (Swiss psychiatrist—focused on the collective consciousness); Wolfman **Jack** (disc jockey/radio broadcaster); Peter **Jackson** (award-winning film director—*Lord of the Rings* trilogy); Edward **Jenner** (doctor—developed smallpox vaccination)

K is for Kindling

In the first part of this **K** chapter I suggest twelve ways to squash, crush, or *kill* intelligence-building—and each is followed by ideas (people, places, things) that can be used as *kindling* to spark children's creativity and productivity. In the second half of this chapter, I **k**eep going by emphasizing **k**ey **K** words, to **k**ick-start your thinking.

Kindling: What Matters

Fires can burn intensely and merrily, or they can sputter and fizzle. Sometimes parents inadvertently kill children's creativity and productivity. This may not be intentional, but when adults are overly busy or preoccupied, they may become distracted or detached from what's going on and pay less attention to children's efforts. Conversely, some parents are too enmeshed or caught up in whatever their children are doing, not leaving enough room for them to develop self-sufficiency, overcome hardship, or feel the pride and joy of their own achievements.

There's a happy medium between parenting that is too detached and parenting that is overly conscientious—a zone wherein kids can feel comfortable learning to engineer their own way forward, whether their chosen path is paved with rocks or pebbles. (Or weeds. The terms "lawnmower" or "bulldozer" parents are sometimes used to refer to those who mow down or remove anything that might interfere with a child's headway.) Parents who want their children to become self-motivated, resilient, and proficient have to determine when to relinquish control or directives that can potentially smother kids' initiatives. Parents also have to figure out when to let children fire up their own competencies, and when they might benefit from some assistance or reinforcement.

With all that in mind, here are a dozen *killers*. Each point is followed by practical suggestions—*kindling*—to foster children's desire to learn!

1. Killer: SCRUTINY

Kindling: Do you hover like a watchdog? Peering constantly over kids' shoulders can be off-putting. Ensure respectful privacy, ample time and space, quiet interludes, and a show of confidence.

2. Killer: RIGIDITY

Kindling: Avoid setting unnecessary constraints or being close-minded about children's efforts or choices. Think before saying, "*No*" or "*Don't*" or "*You must.*"

3. Killer: IMPATIENCE

Kindling: Try not to push too hard. Learning, creative expression, and productive engagement are like embarking upon quests that take time, effort, and patience. Appreciate when time is of the essence—and when a little forbearance or flexibility might go a long way. (What's the rush?)

4. Killer: DOUBT

Kindling: Show optimism rather than misgivings or skepticism. An upbeat attitude and a positive outlook can be invigorating, and serve to promote creativity and a sense of industry.

5. Killer: ISOLATION

Kindling: Some kids enjoy working independently or may prefer a peaceful spot to a crowded noisy one. However, a solitary milieu can also be a potentially lonely and unproductive place. Encourage kids to connect with friends and others who can offer inspiration, support, and opportunities for meaningful collaboration.

6. Killer: FATIGUE

Kindling: When children get enough rest and relaxation, they're better able to focus, exercise the imagination, and apply themselves. There's nothing like a proper night's sleep. Sleep expert Alanna McGinn shares podcasts and articles about sleep health on her blog, Good Nite, Sleep Site.[50] There's information that's applicable for babies, children, and teens—and adults, too.

7. Killer: INDIFFERENCE

Kindling: A sense of purpose is far better than apathy and disengagement. Help kids generate and sustain excitement and curiosity about the world around them. Encourage their involvement in project-based applications and real problem-solving activities. Research shows that greater purpose in life is modifiable, and that it's linked to better health and well-being.[51] (And, it can help protect against cognitive decline in older adults!) So be purposeful—and encourage children to be purposeful, too.

8. Killer: LITTLE OR NO PROGRESS

Kindling: Even a taste of sweet success can be motivating. To facilitate successful outcomes, offer children constructive reinforcement, suggest some helpful foundational information, or provide evidence of headway.

9. Killer: UNFAIR EXPECTATIONS

Kindling: Co-create goals that are manageable, reasonable, and attainable. Children who have a hand in setting sensible, fair, appropriately challenging, and achievable objectives for themselves are more likely to work toward completing them.

10. Killer: COMPLEXITY

Kindling: Lighting too many fires at once can be detrimental—as in too hot to handle. Kids who have to deal with too much at once can become overwhelmed or experience burn out. Simplicity is often the key to success.

11. Killer: LACK OF PROVISIONS

Kindling: Kids may need preparation, support, downtime, supplies, or incentives in order to progress. Or, they may need help with organizational skills, or work habits. Consider what *your* child requires in order to feel ready, and able to move on happily from there.

12. Killer: LACK OF CONFIDENCE

Kindling: Convey faith in children's capabilities. Confidence happens when kids feel respected, connected, and competent. Choice, resourcefulness, and assistance can also be beneficial, helping kids to embrace a more empowering sense of self. We all need a boost now and then!

The 15 additional ideas below all start with the letter **K**. Let them inspire you and your kids.

○ **K**nowledge—this is an essential component of intelligence-building, and creativity, too. However, for the record, there's a difference between knowledge and being smart. Knowledge is knowing what bears are, and that they roam in the woods. Being smart is knowing what to do when you're hiking, and you see one!

○ **K**aleidoscope—a topsy-turvy, colorful, unusual, interesting conglomeration of designs; a visual stimulus that's fun to see, manipulate, and create. Experiencing a single dimension can be restrictive, whereas experiencing many as overlapping and unusual spurs intelligence and creativity at its finest.

○ **K**etchup—the mundane can be livened up. My 8-year-old granddaughter puts ketchup on practically everything because she thinks it tastes better that way. We all have preferences for making things appealing, more lively, interesting, or fun. What's your ketchup?

○ **K**ids—as adults we sometimes forget that kids have fresh and unique ways of looking at the world, and that we can learn from their ideas and alternative points of view.

○ **K**icker—I took Latin in high school, and every Friday our teacher, Mr. Klemencic (which, coincidentally starts with **K**), gave us a quiz. He called it a "kicker." Now, as an educator, I understand that the quiz helped him ascertain what we knew, what we still needed to learn, and what he should focus on in class during the following week. "*Perfer et obdura; dolar hic tibi proderit olim.*" (Be patient and tough. Some day this pain will be useful to you.) Or, perhaps more to the point, "*Sine labore nihil.*" (Nothing without work.)

○ Even **K**eel—it's not just about boats. It's about balance—social-emotional and academic—and in all areas of life. Kindling children's abilities happens best when they have a sense of stability and self-assurance, and the sense that they can weather a storm. Kids are still learning how to do that. Ann Douglas' two *Parenting Through the Storm* books offer parents many encouraging ideas for doing likewise. She discusses children's mental health challenges, learning disorders, and other issues—and also the stress, worry, heartache and feelings that parents wrestle with sometimes. Most importantly, she provides stabilizing strategies to get everyone back on an even keel. Her newest book, *Happy Parents, Happy Kids* is for all parents who seek to fully embrace the joys of parenting and family life.[52]

○ **K**een—this word has many meanings including strong, powerful, sharpened, profound, lively, and eager. Modeling keenness, and encouraging it in children, will take them further as they strive to reach their goals.

○ **K**angaroo—talk about preparedness! This animal has its own built-in knapsack to carry its young and keep it from harm. And, it's a super handy vantage point so a little one can observe its surroundings and learn what to do (and not do) while growing up. Alas, humans don't have the same facility, but we certainly have devised lots of strategies for safe and supportive child-rearing. Being prepared is essential for parenting—and it's also a prerequisite for being smart.

○ **K**ilimanjaro, Tanzania—in October 2012, I was in a small plane and saw this mountain up close. It broke through the clouds, and it was a beautiful and memorable sight. My friend's daughter has climbed more than 19,000 ft. to the peak. She pushed herself to new heights, literally, in so many ways. She saw a lot, learned a great deal, and raised money for charity, too. And, she kindled pride among family and friends. Let's continue to challenge ourselves, and one another.

○ **K**ick in the "But" (with one **T**)—there are many reasons or excuses not to do something. For example, "*But I don't feel well… But it's too hard… But I don't care…*" When this happens to you, give yourself a kick in the but. Demonstrate resolve. (See *Bust Your BUTS: Tips for Teens Who Procrastinate*. In that book I provide information on 28 different buts, and hundreds of strategies so kids can bust them.)

○ **K**nuckle down—something to try if you're having a hard time getting past the buts.

○ **K**nack—a knack for something is an ability, talent, or aptitude. What do your children have a knack for? Photography? Cybernetics? Calligraphy? Gymnastics? Crossword puzzles? Dance? And, what are they doing to pursue their interests? Like most everything else, it will require effort if it is to become a real and enduring strength.

○ **K**eys—parenting is a multifaceted responsibility. Here are four keys: (a) keep children safe; (b) encourage their interests, strengths, and creativity—and help them find opportunities to pursue them; (c) listen and maintain open channels of communication; and (d) be available to offer support and guidance as needed. What keys unlock the finest possibilities for your child?

○ **K**inesthetic—refers to strength in movement, bodily motions, and fine motor control. Kinetic energy is the energy of motion—a turning wheel, a pulsating waterfall, a shooting star. Some kids learn best by participating in physical experiences because they find this energizes the mind and body. Give kids plenty of opportunities to develop their kinesthetic capabilities.

○ **K**indness—Author Henry James said, *"Three things in human life are important: The first is to be kind; the second is to be kind; and the third is to be kind."* Perhaps the fourth is to help children appreciate the importance of this, and to encourage them to kindle kindness whenever they can.

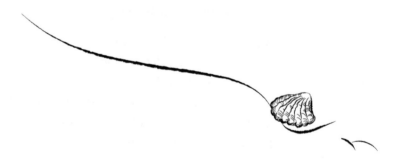

L is for Learning

One might expect *"L is for Learning"* to be the likely lead for a list of letter **L** words about encouraging children's high-level abilities. However, let's look at **load**—when to tread **lightly**, and also what requires **lots** more consideration (that is, when to leap liberally).

Learning: What Matters

Is learning about following passions, or is it a skill that develops over time with practice and hard work?

The answer to this question may lie in the view that passion and skill are *both* important in order for children to broaden their intelligence and enrich their lives. People learn by:

a. being open to figuring out new things, including actively engaging in problem-solving strategies,

b. having good supports and models, including parents and teachers who offer guidance, and

c. having plentiful opportunities to try and to practice different learning processes, including cultivating joy in those processes, one step at a time.

Learning is about enthusiasm and effort. It's a progression, and it occurs incrementally. It involves different kinds of thinking—creative, critical, focused, and more relaxed or broad-based—and it involves being *flexible* about thinking, and having the *desire* to think. It may also involve elation or frustration; excitement or reservation; surges forward or procrastination; the use of visual memory or past experience; spontaneity or careful premeditation.

Learning is a relatively permanent change in thought or behavior. It is not preprogrammed—it occurs as a result of experience, and stimulation. Learning is what education is all about. However, the best classrooms are not only in schools, and don't necessarily include a teacher. Life itself, including interactions with others, stimulating environments, opportunity, choice, and also thinking about the experiences one has, can promote learning and extend it.

Learning involves reflection—that is, being able to recognize and deal with the kinds of constraints and factors that hinder learning (such as resistance, distractions, and difficulty communicating), and the provisions and factors that help learning (such as using the imagination, synthesizing ideas, and participating in hands-on activities). It's important to encourage children to develop and hone communication and language skills, because these facilitate thought. And, children can be helped to appreciate that change will also inevitably have an impact on their learning as they grow and mature. They will begin to see their world differently as they continue to explore, come to terms with it, develop skills, and follow and also create new pathways.

If we think about learning as "*a smorgasbord of processes*," then we need to think carefully about what is on offer. The smorgasbord descriptor is used by Scott Barry Kaufman (Scientific Director of the Imagination Institute), in his podcast interview with author, engineer, and researcher Barbara Oakley wherein they discuss practices and tools that help people learn.[53] Kaufman states, "*There needs to be more creativity in academia across the board*." Oakley concurs, and she describes how people can improve their learning, tap their potential, and use change advantageously. (Check out her book *Mindshift: Break Through Obstacles to Learning and Discover Your Hidden Passions*.) Kaufman also suggests that, "*More than curriculum, it is important to ask students questions about their dreams, passions, and how they imagine themselves to be when they grow up, as 'catalysers' for achievement*."

So, help kids reach for horizons! When they play, reflect, and explore new attitudes, methods, technologies, and opportunities for learning, those horizons broaden exponentially.

In this chapter, **L** words are linked to aspects of learning that parents and teachers can consider as they support children's development and help to extend their reach.

Think "Lightly"

○ **L**abels—don't emphasize labels—gifted or other. And, it's better to label programs rather than children. Try and look past any label and pay attention to the *child*, and the specific needs he or she might have in one or more areas. Sometimes those needs can be lost behind an individual's categorical designation. Other times there's more focus on the similarities among those within a certain category, and less attention paid to differences or individual strengths and weaknesses. Although gifted labelling can be affirming, and be like a ticket of admission for access to special programs, there are also potential drawbacks to such labeling. These can include self-doubts, inaccuracy, overly-high expectations, elitism, sudden program transitions, envy and rejection by peers, feelings of differentness, arrogance, and even complacency. Use labels carefully. They're meant for packing crates, not for kids.

○ **L**ean—children may be inclined to rely on their parents when difficulties arise. The extent of their dependence will differ at various age and maturity levels, and in relation to context and circumstances, including time and place. Reliance is okay, to a point. Umbilical cords are supposed to be cut. Help children forge their way toward autonomy.

○ **L**ead—those pathways will be less onerous if you first share the lead, knowing when to relinquish it as kids demonstrate that they can take responsibility for and by themselves.

○ **L**ayer—learning is not lickety-split. It's a process that involves building on what one already knows, often little by little, or layer upon layer. This requires time, and hard work.

○ **L**uck—sometimes things fall into place—like the right learning opportunity at just the right time, or the perfect constellation of factors that enables people to solve a tough problem. If luck isn't on their side, people can be proactive, prayerful, reflective, planful, collaborative, and smart. As opposed to relying on horse-shoes, wishbones, four leaf clovers, or crossed fingers.

○ **L**aurels and **L**ollipops—it's not prudent to overload kids with accolades or to indulge them with rewards. It's far more productive to offer genuine praise for their efforts, when earned.

○ **L**agniappe—a small gift or a little something extra that someone acquires every once in a while, often unexpectedly, and for good measure. It can be motivating and, like the 13th donut in a box, it can be a treat.

○ **L**inks—there are endless online learning possibilities and resources. For example, blogs, TED talks, articles, podcasts, videos, webinars, and videoconferences. Use them prudently. However, by way of example, there are several dozen links listed in the endnotes of this book, including an article with 100 different resources for gifted learners such as coding and programming; photography and videography; performing arts; environmental and life science; math; engineering, aviation; music; and more.[54] And, one good link inevitably leads to others…

○ **L**ock-step—children don't develop in lock-step with one another. This is true even among those who seem very much alike. Thus parenting is neither predictable nor routine. Be prepared to deviate, and to show a little give and take.

○ **L**oosen—release the safety net, a bit at a time. Give kids liberties as they develop the ability to handle them. Be lenient but not so laid-back as to be lax or liable to compromise their welfare.

Think "Lots"

○ **L**ove—unconditionally.

○ **L**isten—be available whenever children want to share their thoughts, concerns, achievements, aspirations, or anything else. Listen attentively in order to learn, to better understand kids' feelings, and to be able to respond effectively. Ancient Greek philosopher Epictetus was wise to note, *"We have two ears and one mouth so that we can listen twice as much as we speak."*

○ **L**abor—success demands work. Model it. Encourage it. Support it. Reinforce it.

○ **L**ife skills—the competences we use every day. For example, communication, emotional literacy, social interaction, personal care. And more... These skills are important at every age. For strategies to help kids thrive, visit Marlaine Cover's informative Parenting 2.0 website.[55]

○ **L**ook—seek out and take advantage of local and long-range liaisons and leads for learning. This might include courses, seminars, conferences (gifted-related and other kinds), panel discussions, chat groups, and book clubs. Find out what's available in your area, or what's accessible online. Also, watch for books on a variety of seminal topics. For example, in *Bright, Talented, and Black: A Guide for Families of African American Gifted Learners*, Joy L. Davis offers information, guidelines, and practical strategies for parenting and educating black gifted learners, and she offers resources for minority gifted students. If you're curious about how gifted learners will fare in the future, there's Tijl Koenderink's *Bright Futures for Bright Minds*. There are new, and also updated books on twice exceptional learners, summer programs, advocacy, behavioral issues, coding, leadership, differentiation—you name it. Just look!

○ **L**augh—a smile is universal, and so is laughter. Give freely.

○ **L**essons—they teach us how to be better at living our lives. Lessons can happen anytime, anywhere. Model receptivity by showing kids that you're always open to learning. For example, on the online site Savvy Mom, Executive Editor, Rebecca Eckler, offers some shrewd *"lessons for modern day parents."*[56] These include how to demonstrate that success has many guises, help kids deal with boredom, make hugs last longer, show why consequences matter, and play *"rose and thorn"* (discussing the best and worst part of each day) so children come to realize that all manner of experiences are like lessons that can enable people to understand things.

○ **L**ikability—do what you like, like what you do, and encourage children to do likewise.

○ **L**iteracy and **L**anguage—the basis for developing communication skills, and the foundation for knowledge acquisition—*so* important for lifelong learning.

○ **L**ogic—necessary in order to make sense of the world, and to function effectively within it. Starting in infancy, and continuing on from there...

○ **L**atitude and **L**eniency—show tolerance, patience, and broadmindedness, all of which will pay large dividends as children learn these traits, and exhibit them, too.

○ **L**imits—know them, respect them, and perhaps even push them but in ways that are comfortable and meaningful. See the book *Pushing the Limits: How Schools Can Prepare Our Children of Today for the Challenges of Tomorrow* by Kelly Gallagher and Nancy Steinhauer.

○ **L**uxury—cherish the time you spend with your child and make the moments count. Kids grow up so quickly!

○ **L**ast but not **L**east... **L**iveliness—it's that dynamic, energetic "joie de vivre" that can spark and invigorate learning all across the lifespan.

M is for Motivation

M marks the **m**idpoint of the alphabet, whereupon **my** mission is to **m**indfully **m**anage a **m**osaic of **m**otivators. Within this **m**ix I include **m**any **m**astery-oriented ones, that lead toward **m**eaningful under-standings, and other **m**otivators that are also **m**obilizing but **m**ore **m**ainstay—that is, **m**oderate albeit not **m**undane. Life is filled with **m**yriad **m**uddles and **m**ind-boggling **m**ysteries that **m**otivated **m**inds can help **m**itigate. Be part of the ***motivation*** movement! Marshal, muster, and **m**ove!

Here are my **m**usings about what **m**atters, followed by **m**aterial on: 1) ***making the most of momentum***, 2) ***more momentum***, and 3) ***maximum momentum***.

Motivation: What Matters

The literature on motivation is so crammed with theories and research findings that it can be difficult for parents to get to the root of it all. However, two important points stand out.

1) In order to maximize children's motivation (and sustain it!) parents and teachers have to ensure that tasks are *suitable*—both manageable enough to do and challenging enough to be worth doing.

2) These tasks have to be *relevant*, or why should kids bother? Authentic connections between what children already know, and what is being asked of them can be motivating, leading to deeper levels of thinking, and making activities and demands more interesting and engaging.

In addition to suitability and relevance, consider the importance of rein-forcement, realizable goals, innovative and integrated tasks, appropriate pacing, fun, choice, and the opportunity to be creative.

Children who are not motivated, or who have trouble staying on task, are not likely to realize their full capabilities. When kids forsake their skills or limit their efforts, they end up sabotaging their ability to attain goals, and to experience the pleasures of achievement. Sometimes difficulties or failures create shaky ground and disappointment, which can get in the way of forward momentum. That's when it's especially important to help children gain a firm footing, relinquish self-doubts, embrace a strong work ethic, and forge ahead.

With that in mind, parents can encourage kids to take a mastery-oriented approach. What exactly does that mean? And what does it have to do with motivation and gifted/high-ability learners?

Mastery-oriented learners don't give up when facing difficulty. They dig in, they focus on improving their performance, and they recognize the value of learning for the sake of learning, even when an experience is taxing. They monitor their own progress so they can see signs—even small steps—of advancement as it occurs. A mastery orientation helps people overcome negativity about tasks (such as feelings relating to inadequacy, stress, worry, or fear), so they become more positive, confident, and motivated. Even the strongest and most capable learners can experience times when they lack initiative. However, understanding and mastery can motivate people to accomplish even more, leading to new skills, augmented proficiencies, joy, and gratification.

In order to fuel the development of skills and knowledge, children have to *want* to invest their time and energy. To that end, a sense of accomplishment can be a powerful motivator. And, because each individual has a personal profile of abilities, those accomplishments will vary across time, situations, and domains. Ensure that expectations are reasonable. Remember that small successes matter. They lead to larger ones, they can be motivating, and they help kids feel good about themselves—from the inside out.

Intrinsic motivation is a drive from within. It can spark a search for information, stimulate further curiosity, and generate action. Intrinsic motivators include feelings of pride, competence, and internalized values such as diligence and integrity. Tasks that require conjecture, investigation, high-order or divergent thinking may be more intrinsically motivating for gifted learners. They will likely have little interest in activities that involve basic applications, memorization, or simple responses.

Extrinsic motivation refers to incentives or external factors like happy face stickers, grades, applause, or praise. These, along with opportunities to succeed, and recognition of progress, can reinforce and stimulate children's efforts. Extrinsic motivation can help build self-esteem—and lead to intrinsic motivation. Helping children cultivate a growth mindset about the nature of intelligence, understanding it as being incremental and not fixed, is another way to increase intrinsic motivation.

Gifted learners typically prefer tasks that will advance their knowledge, and lead to challenging learning goals and new skills. However, specific learning issues can interfere with children's motivation. These issues include frustration and boredom; disabilities; fear of failure or success; academic overload; distractions; lack of self-confidence; weak study skills or work habits; and a variety of possible social, emotional, academic or other concerns that may be particular to any one child or family, and that might require address before motivation kicks in. Pay attention to children's previous experiences and motivators; the environment; health and well-being; problem behaviors; attitudes; and individual qualities and preferences.

Inspiration lies at the heart of motivation. Encourage children's curiosity and support them as they pursue different interests. Lighten up and be patient as they explore their world. Curiosity is a powerful motivator.

Other motivational tips? When children sense that others have confidence in them they're more motivated to invest in learning. Offer direct, immediate feedback, and praise effort. Offer variety. Offer reassurance in the form of words and gestures if things get bogged down, and help kids appreciate that an effortful task can feel good. Offer a reality-check about rationales for rules and restrictions, and help kids understand these. Offer assistance with goal-setting. Children who perceive the adults in their lives as being available, caring, patient, and willing to assist are more motivated to learn.

Making the Most of Momentum

○ **M**eaningfulness—motivation is often associated with triggers such as need, instinct, curiosity, or encouragement. Learning opportunities should be interesting so kids can experience the kind of motivation that comes from personal engagement.

○ **M**emory—past experiences can motivate people by affirming what they know and what they can already do, readying them for additional memorable challenges.

○ **M**ystery—life is full of mysteries, however being smart shouldn't be one of them. Abilities develop over time with plenty of opportunities to learn. If learning is the engine of intelligence, then motivation is the engine of learning.

○ **M**arshmallows, **M&M**'s, **M**uffins—at a basic level, motivators might be candy, rewards, or gold stars. At a more mature or sophisticated level, motivators might include sparking interest, offering hands-on activities, setting tough but realizable goals, and fostering self-regulation.

○ **M**onday **M**ornings—a downer? A fresh start? Depends… What's your mindset?

○ **M**indset—success depends on many factors, including perseverance, and a willingness to confront obstacles. This is also known as a "growth mindset." People who have a growth mindset understand that learning happens step by step, and that intelligence develops systematically over time through effort. For more on this, see Carol Dweck's book *Mindset: The New Psychology of Success* wherein the author explains why acquiring and sustaining a growth mindset is integral to learning.

○ **M**aybe?—that's too mild-mannered. Think, "Why not? Author A.A. Milne wrote, *"Promise me you'll always remember: You're braver than you believe, stronger than you seem, and smarter than you think."*

○ **M**ental acuity—mental acuity implies sharpness or keen perception. (There's also visual, and auditory acuity.) Being perceptive is advantageous because it helps people understand and respond more effectively to sensory stimuli, different perspectives, and problems. When kids are aware and alert it can contribute to their acuity, and their motivation.

○ **M**atch—expectations are more readily met when tasks and ability match. Parents and children can advocate for good programming matches. If a child lacks motivation, explore different avenues and resources. Try incorporating music, art, or drama into activities. Or inject fun, suspense, mystery, or controversy. Make it matter, and it will be motivating!

○ **M**arks—some kids are motivated by high marks, whereas others are moved to improve by mediocre or even low ones. Help kids find their mark by offering a supportive emotional climate. "*You can do it! Hooray!*" And if, for example, schools only teach to tests, and if teachers only focus on that rather narrow aspect of student learning, children run the risk of missing out on a whole range of understandings and motivating ideas. (How sad.)

○ **M**others—no list of **M** words about motivation would be complete without mentioning mothers—and fathers—as major role models for their children. Sherlyn Pang Luedtke's book *The Mommy Advantage* offers helpful insights on parenthood, commitment to family, self-care, and personal growth. And check out the suggestions in Rebecca Eane's newest book, *The Gift of a Happy Mother.*

More Momentum

○ **M**indfulness—kids can learn about the invigorating power of being in the moment by taking time to pause and become more in tune with the mind, body, senses, and surroundings. This will help them become more appreciative of the here and now, and less reactive to and overwhelmed by life's stressors. Many schools incorporate mindfulness programs into the curriculum. There are also all kinds of resources on mindfulness. A good starting point is the non-profit Mindful website with articles and videos about healthy minds and healthy lives.[57]

○ **M**ountain climbing—no, not everyone can scale monumental heights. But everyone *can* set manageable goals and work mightily to attain them.

○ **M**onitor and **M**odify—discover and provide the right pacing, structure, feedback, and focus. Then keep it going. Sometimes a child does not receive proper educational programming or service provisions because, for example, there may be dual exceptionality, or behavioral or other concerns. It's important to understand what underlies a child's struggles. Once causality is identified, circumstances can be ameliorated with the right supports, encouragements, resources, and strategies for addressing the challenges. There's substantial information about this in *Misdiagnosis and Dual Diagnoses of Gifted Children and Adults* (2nd Edition) by Webb., J. T.; Amend, E. R.; Beljan, P.; Webb, N. E.; Kuzujanakis, M.; Olenchak, R.; and Goerss, J.

○ **M**ix it up—make learning experiences interesting, different, novel, rousing!

○ **M**usic—A melody, minstrel, or movie can inspire. So can motion, like Zumba or dance. Music resonates for people of every age, and there are benefits relating to brain development, motion, relaxation, play, and creative expression.[58] A noteworthy musical site with songs and learning experiences for little ones is Nancy Kopman's Children's Music with a Purpose.[59] And, for an instrumental experience for would-be composers, visit Hanne Deneire's Children Are Composers.[60]

○ **M**ythology—stories, folklore, legends, fables, and tales of yore all offer moving accounts of a mélange of characters motivated by means and miscellaneous methods. (Hercules has been mentioned. There are Marvel characters, and more.)

○ **M**eeting others—chat, co-create, work together, share ideas. See where it leads. Some folks may be in the mood for a meeting, or merry make-believe, or meandering in a museum. What's your pleasure?

○ **M**oney/**M**arketability—an eye on the future, including career goals and financial stability, can be motivating, especially for adolescents and young adults. Kids can explore different career paths, talk to counselors, determine prerequisites, and do a little planning for what lies ahead.

○ **M**entors—great possibilities for learning and doing, and to complement and extend curriculum! Children may be interested in playing an instrument, designing a robot, becoming entrepreneurial, or furthering curiosity about a trade or vocation. To learn more about mentorships for kids, a good starting point is the National Mentoring Partnership.[61] Or see "Mentoring and Kids" at *The Creativity Post*.[62]

Maximum Momentum

○ **M**istakes and **M**eltdowns—help kids understand that resilience is important, that wrangling success from failure is a learning process, and that they *can* find the fortitude necessary to keep going if demands and responsibilities become daunting. Theodore Roosevelt said, "*It is hard to fail but it is worse never to have tried to succeed.*"

○ **M**avericks—encourage children to become frontrunners—to find their way and make a difference. Provide guidance, and reassurance.

○ **M**arvel—tap into the senses—touch, taste, smell, hearing, and sight. Seize and appreciate them. The many wonders of the world can motivate emotions and thought!

○ **M**oral compass—a tried and true tool for directional strength, for character development, and for forging pathways toward success at home, school, and elsewhere.

○ **M**easurable—it's helpful when goals and interim accomplishments are not vague, when achievements are measurable, and when children and teens can gauge their progress.

○ **M**etacognition—it has to do with thinking about thinking, for example by engaging in and modeling inquiry and reflection. This directs attention, supports self-determination and autonomy, and can be a motivating means to an end.

○ **M**eteoric—forward momentum doesn't have to dazzle. Maintaining balance, peace of mind, happiness, and well-being matter most.

N is for Nurturing

> I now navigate **N** words, with a **n**od to all those who **n**obly **n**urture children's high-level development in accordance with their **n**umerous **n**eeds. In a **n**utshell, here are 1) *necessities*, and 2) *nuances* to think about…

Nurturing: What Matters

Nurturing facilitates growth, development, and success. At a basic level, it involves offering protection, food and water, and a place to live.

Nurturing children to thrive involves paying careful attention to their needs, throughout the many formative years, and preferably on an ongoing basis. Whether these needs relate to safety, schooling, emotional or social intelligence, or something else, it's up to parents to determine what is required to help their child grow, and how best to proceed at any point in time. It's an incremental process, one day at a time. Some steps are well-defined and straight forward, whereas others are more speculative, and roundabout. Some measures are subtle, and others are bold. Some pathways are well-illuminated and others less so. The following ideas about necessities and nuances offer parents some direction.

Necessities (the nitty-gritty…)

○ **N**etworks—friends, families, colleagues—we depend upon one another, locally and globally, for ideas, recommendations, updates, findings, and strategies. For example, the National Association for Gifted Children (NAGC),[63] and Supporting the Emotional Needs of the Gifted (SENG),[64] are two noteworthy organizations based in the US, and with affiliates elsewhere. Their members embrace and further the mandate to help kids reach the highest cognitive levels possible while also tending to other critical aspects of their development. Readers can scan the substantial resources online and discover social networks, webinars, and conference opportunities.

○ **N**eighbors—another integral part of a supportive network. Our communities are strongholds for children's optimal growth. "*It takes a village to raise a child.*" (This is a popular African proverb. It was adopted by Hillary Clinton for her book, "*It Takes a Village: And Other Lessons Children Teach Us.*")

○ **N**ascent—each child has promise—talents and abilities that will emerge with maturity, and with the right kinds of learning opportunities, and nurturing.

○ **N**eural plasticity—the brain continually changes in its structure and functional pathways, sculpted by experiences across the lifespan. Scientific research shows that intensive brain-building occurs during the early years, and again during early adolescence, influencing and shaping children's development. For more on this, see *Age of Opportunity: Lessons from the New Science of Adolescence* by Laurence Steinberg. (The author offers compelling information about the brain, particularly during the early teenage years, ages 11 to 14). Necessities for brain health include opportunities for playful exploration, conversation, and exposure to many kinds of cognitive and sensory stimulation.

○ **N**eurodiversity—this term refers to neurological differences, or differences in the way the brain functions. These human variations should be recognized and respected. Each person is a complex entity, and no two individuals are exactly the same cognitively, environmentally, genetically, and so on. Research is shedding light on new neuroscientific understandings relating to differences among gifted learners, including physiology, implications, learning, mental health—and cautions. The body and brain work together as people experience life, and therefore both must be considered when supporting children's development.

○ **N**etscapes—new technological advances continue to alter the status quo, and affect the ways we acquire information, communicate, and learn. Help children develop technological know-how, and teach them to use it wisely.

○ **N**aïve—don't be. As long as there've been kids, there've been parents looking out for them! Observe, listen, model, guide, motivate, and be nearby when needed. If you think your job is done, then think again.

○ **N**otice—keep your eyes open for little things as well as big ones. Sometimes small matters end up becoming challenging issues that might have been nipped in the bud.

○ **N**arrow—kids who narrowly miss a designated cut-off for inclusion in a gifted program likely have advanced learning needs that require address. Differentiated programming would be beneficial. In fact, it would be beneficial for *all* students. (Lannie Kanevsky writes about the importance of differentiation practices, as well as effective approaches. She is the author of the *Tool Kit for High End Curriculum Differentiation*.)

○ **N**ever—never stop advocating for gifted/high-ability learners. If you don't advocate—and help kids learn to advocate for themselves—who will?

○ **N**ucleus—offer safety, learning experiences, direction, and reassurance, ideally within the nucleus and warm embrace of a loving family.

Nuances (nevertheless, don't neglect...)

○ **N**ewsworthy vs **N**onsense—be astute when it comes to determining what child-rearing information merits your close attention, and what should be taken lightly.

○ **N**egotiation—it's somewhat of an art. Especially when temperaments clash or emotions run high. Be sensible. Avoid power struggles—with kids, teachers, or others who may not necessarily agree with you. And, don't be too quick to say "no." (On the other hand, sometimes "no" IS warranted or even necessary. Have a look at Susan Newman's *The Book of No: 365 Ways to Say It and Mean It.* Then you'll be better able to figure out what merits a "yes," a "no," or a "maybe...")

○ **N**ormal—what's normal? What's not? Every child is different. Some have strengths with numeracy, or numbers; some are naughty, or nerdy, or neat, or noisy, or neglectful, or nonstop questioners. Others are still finding their personal nexus or niche.

○ **N**agging—kids often need reminders, however don't needle or nitpick. If you want some helpful parental coaching on topics such as picky eating, sibling rivalry, tantrums, and more, see Nicole Schwarz's blog on the Imperfect Families website.[65]

○ **N**ap—rest is important. A balance of stimulation and downtime is good over the long-term.

○ **N**otions—children have all kinds of curious, novel, and even outlandish ideas. The future depends on creativity and progress. Why be a naysayer?

○ **N**egativity—children (and adults) can learn to overcome negativity by developing inner strengths and focusing on positive experiences. That sounds like a tall order! However, neuropsychologist Rick Hanson writes and speaks about "negativity bias" (which he says is like "*a bottleneck in the brain*"), and he provides strategies for taking in good experiences and gradually incorporating them into the way the brain works. To learn more about how to get rid of negativity, and to discover how mental activity can change brain structure in positive ways, listen to his TED talk on this.[66] And, in his book *Resilient* (coauthored with his son), he discusses twelve specific inner strengths that can help to diminish negative feelings and actions, and increase contentment and personal growth.

○ **N**erve—the word brings to mind synonyms like courage, boldness, spunk, and bravado. Nelson Mandela said, "*It always seems impossible until it's done.*" No matter how you define a child's spirit of adventure, it shouldn't be nixed.

O is for Opportunities

> Children's learning **opportunities** can be **o**rdinary or **o**utstanding.
> Here's an **o**verview of my **o**wn **o**pinions for **o**ptimizing them.

○ **O**ld-fashioned—listening, chatting, reading together, playing games—these aren't new-fangled ideas. They're old-fashioned, tried-and true, and important ways to foster children's development.

○ **O**riginality—encourage it! Outrageous, obscure, odd or offbeat ideas can often be springboards for exciting new outcomes.

○ **O**logy—astrology, biology, cryptology, zoology—from **A** to **Z**, there are many different "*ologies*" (or forms of knowledge) that might capture children's interest. Help them find and pursue resources, programs, activities, and mentors.

○ **O**utings and field trips—excursions can be fun and also quality learning experiences, enabling children to broaden their perspectives. These trips can be aligned with school curriculum, and they can open new avenues of interest. *The Henry Ford* website offers guidelines and helpful resources for planning field trips.[67]

○ **O**pen-mindedness—learning opportunities can occur at any time, in any place—often, occasionally, real or virtual.

○ **O**bvious—it's clear that as tech-boundaries continue to expand so, too, does the need to be discerning, and to oversee how children utilize these outlets and online venues.

○ **O**nline venues—increasingly, technology informs what people do and what they know, and there are countless apps, links, tools, and portals for extended learning by children, and by adults. However, parents have to caution children that there are also online venues that are not well-intentioned. Safety is paramount. Parents can teach kids boundaries, investigate the installation of child-friendly and safe search engines, underscore the importance of not posting personal information or sharing passwords, and monitor when and how children use computers, tablets, phones, and other electronic devices.

○ **O**verexcitabilities—sometimes children experience intensities in certain areas relating to their intellectual, psychomotor, imaginative, sensual, or emotional functioning. It's good to be aware of this, especially when thinking about what kinds of learning opportunities are best suited for any one child. Kazimierz Dabrowski researched overexcitabilities. (For information on his work, see Sal Mendaglio's book *Dabrowski's Theory of Positive Disintegration*.) To discover more about emotional intensity and sensitivity, see *Living with Intensity: Understanding the Sensitivity, Excitability, and Emotional Development of Gifted Children, Adolescents, and Adults* by Susan Daniels and Michael Piechowski. However, if a smart child is depressed, intensely emotional, or overly sensitive, don't simply assume or conclude that this is just part of what "being gifted" is all about.[68] Find out what might be underlying or contributing to feelings and behaviors. A change of environment or circumstances can often be helpful—for example, less bullying or pressure; more listening or play or suitable challenge; and possibly the support of others such as good friends, a trusted mentor, a counsellor, or a therapist.

○ **O**rganization skills—if kids aren't organized then lots of options, even the most captivating ones, can seem overwhelming. Help children become adept at managing their time, materials, and techno-activity. See Mitzi Weinman's book *It's About Time! Transforming Chaos into Calm, A to Z.*

○ **O**pposition—healthy opposition is useful for appreciating other people's perspectives. Teach kids the benefits of controversy, debate, and deliberation, all of which will enhance their thinking and learning.

○ **O**verabundance—too much of anything is generally not good. Kids sometimes need assistance recognizing this so that opportune times remain opportune, not onerous.

○ **O**bservation—keep your eyes open to ensure that children are feeling comfortable with their schooling and other experiences, and that challenges are not too easy, and not too hard. Observing is as important as listening (they are complementary), and sometimes even more important than speaking.

○ **O**bjectives—help kids set reasonable goals—ones they can orchestrate, and that are attainable within a realistic time frame.

○ **O**fferings—aside from conventional school curriculum, think about community centers, extracurricular programs, mentorship arrangements, and specialty focus workshops (for example, in the arts, such as origami, opera, or oil painting). Kids can seek and find leadership, research, and internship programs in their areas of interest. There are also opportunities for children of various ages to enrol in courses that focus on strengthening mental health and well-being. For example, Kids Now is a proactive Canadian organization that offers free after school programs that have helped thousands of early adolescents learn to cope with challenges, and develop life skills, confidence, healthy relationships, and smart ways of transitioning to high school.[69] What's offered in your neighborhood?

○ **O**ptimism—a positive attitude can help make okay experiences even better.

P is for Productivity

I **p**refer **p**aragraph form for **p**resenting **p**erspectives **p**ertaining to **p**athways toward ***productivity***—and I **p**epper the **p**iece with **p**ractical **p**ointers for **p**arents. **P**ertinent headings include: 1) ***planning and preparation***, 2) ***proper programming***, 3) ***play***, 4) ***paying attention***, 5) ***possible problems***, and 6) ***practice and persistence***. **P**lus, **p**lease have a **p**eek at the **p**lentiful **p**ostscript I **p**rovide just for young **p**eople!

Planning and Preparation

The first step to anywhere may be the hardest. It helps to figure out where you're headed, and what you'll require on the journey and in order to get to the destination. And, of course, paths have a way of diverging. *Planning* involves thinking in advance about goals, and *preparation* involves investigating and acquiring the resources and supports you might need.

Both planning and preparation require time, effort, and thought—but planning and preparation are worth it because they enable people to anticipate and take steps forward, and to respond more purposefully to occurrences, tasks, and responsibilities. It's good to show kids strategies that will help them to become better planners and learn to prepare themselves, so they can aspire to be successful and productive.

Proper Programming

Children are more responsive when they're asked to participate in meaningful activities. This requires thoughtful attention to what fits a given individual in a particular situation. The best learning programs are those that are designed or adapted for children's interests and levels of readiness, aligned with their areas of strength and weakness. If you want to foster and sustain a child's engagement and productivity, aim for a creative and motivating approach, set and co-create clearly defined expectations, and remember to be flexible around pacing or other circumstances along the way.

Play

Play provides children with opportunities to develop skills that will be needed for achievement and fulfillment over the long haul. Unstructured play is a cost-effective investment in a child's development, requiring little more than time, space, and imagination. It's important to encourage kids to create their own fun, discover what they like to do, and pursue their interests. Play is a forerunner for intelligence, creativity, and productivity. Moreover, through play, children learn how to process and effectively cope with their feelings, get along well with others, "*shake their sillies out,*"[70] and enjoy the great outdoors. And, the beautiful thing about playtime is that one never gets too old for it! (See also "**E**arly learning" within this book for more on play—including resources.)

Paying Attention

Know what's happening in your child's life. Listen, observe, communicate openly, and stay on top of things so you're better positioned to advise, guide, and trouble-shoot. Honor children's passions and preferences, give them access to relevant and stimulating learning experiences, help to ensure that they're fittingly challenged, and reinforce their efforts. Don't hover, but do encourage, offer genuine praise, and support their endeavors.

Possible Problems (Such as Procrastination and Perfectionism)

There are many ways of proceeding toward a short, interim, or end goal, yet sometimes things stall or go off the rails. For example, procrastination can impede a person's progress. There may be good reasons why people put things off—just as there may be rather questionable ones. Nevertheless, procrastination can obstruct learning, and short-circuit productivity. To find out more, and for hundreds of practical suggestions for dealing with task avoidance, see my book *Not Now, Maybe Later; Helping Children Overcome Procrastination*. (And, yes, there are tips for adults, too!)

Some children are perfectionistic. They feel compelled to do things just so, always driving themselves toward precision. There are many different reasons for this, too. However, perfectionists may feel overwhelmed by demands, and can become upset and self-critical when a product isn't turning out the way they anticipated. Lisa Van Gemert shares insights on this, and more, in her book *Perfectionism: A Practical Guide to Managing 'Never Good Enough.'* And, Rosemary Callard-Szulgit presents information, questions and answers, and many resources in *Perfectionism and Gifted Children, 2nd Edition.*

Depending upon the situation, and upon what underlies a child's procrastination or perfectionist behavior, there are lots of strategies parents can use to help children become more comfortable with pursuits, and with outcomes. For instance, parents can temper their comments and feedback by being constructive and judicious rather than critical. They can also help kids understand that they shouldn't equate self-worth with achievement. And, it's better to comment on the behavior not the child, recognizing that sometimes children need guidance or practical suggestions to learn to relax and/or redirect their focus.

Practice and Persistence

Parents often tell their children to practice. Whether it's piano chords, swim strokes, math equations, or something else entirely, practice can lead to achievement. Malcolm Gladwell, bestselling author of *Outliers: The Story of Success,* wrote (on page 42), *"Practice isn't the thing you do once you're good. It's the thing you do that makes you good."* However, practice demands resolve, self-discipline, and patience. Attitude matters, too, but—like a strong work ethic—it requires nurturing. Parents, teachers, and others can help children develop a more positive, confident, and resolute outlook by demonstrating how and why practice matters, by being upbeat, by chatting about perseverance, and by adopting a growth mindset. When kids see the adults in their lives learning, working hard, and being resilient, the message conveyed is very clear—effort and commitment are empowering!

Postscript: Positioning the Perspectives...
Pointers Just for Kids!

How to Improve Your Planning and Preparation

○ Get to know yourself, including personal tendencies and work habits relating to the following:
  • prioritizing
  • scheduling
  • knowing what organizational strategies serve you well, and
  • getting the necessary materials for task completion.

○ Make sure expectations are clear. (Fair? Flexible? Realistic? Attainable?)

○ When planning, consider what you can learn from past experiences. For example, think about your previous successes and hurdles, and how much time you usually need to complete things.

○ Consider the counsel of ancient Greek philosopher, Aristotle (384 BC—322 BC), who said, "*Good habits formed at youth make all the difference.*" Look at that date! Those words have stood the test of time!

○ Try to anticipate possible complications, obstacles, and consequences.

○ Be optimistic about what needs to be done and have confidence in your ability to do it.

○ Most accomplishments occur little by little over time. Factor in patience.

How to Overcome Perfectionism

○ Challenge your misconceptions or possible faulty beliefs. What comprises excellence? Why does everything have to be done "just so?"

○ Purposely make a small mistake—slip up or do something imperfectly. (What happens?)

○ View mistakes as learning opportunities that lead to personal growth.

○ Balance criticism by focusing on your accomplishments.

○ Emotions affect how people deal with things. Take note of your feelings. For example, if you're frazzled, take a break and try to relax with breathing exercises, stretching, music, or time out.

○ Be selective about resources, and mindful of the time you spend gathering and using them. Recognize when enough is enough.

○ Set high but realistic standards for yourself. Priorities are learning and experience, *not* performance or product.

How to Overcome Procrastination

○ Concentrate on the value of the task. That is, why it matters.

○ Identify your reason(s) for putting something off. Overwhelmed? Worried? Muddled? Too easy? Too difficult? Don't care? Low energy level? Perhaps your parents, a teacher, or a close friend can help you figure out why you're procrastinating, and also encourage and support your efforts to get on track.

○ Recognize recurring excuses and refusals. Then try to eliminate them.

○ Work constructively with others. Don't try to take on too much alone.

○ Think about what incentives and motivators might work for you. (See "**M** is for Motivation" in this book, and also the many tips in *Bust Your BUTS*.)

○ Commit to action, not avoidance—and then to staying focused. Show that you have the ability to persist when challenged, and try to look forward to the joy of getting things done.

Pivotal Point for Pupils: Consider talking with someone you trust about any concerns or questions you may have related to planning and preparation, perfectionism, or procrastination.

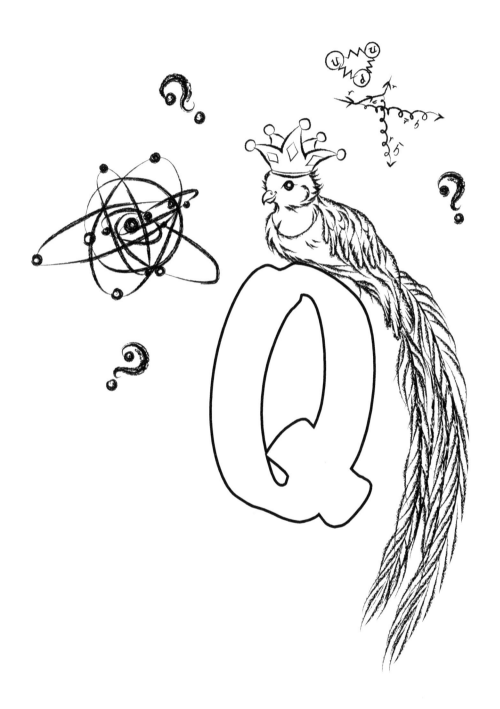

Q is for Questions

For the letter **Q**, I share a few pressing **q**uestions that parents often ask educators and other professionals about children's high-level development. These **q**uestions reflect a desire for **q**uality information about concerns—for example, about supportive measures, issues, interests, and testing. There are answers here—and throughout this book. And, within this letter **Q** segment, I also include a **q**uasi-**q**uiz consisting of several thought-provoking **q**uestions that parents can ask themselves. Finally, I wrap up with some **q**uestions that parents can ask their kids, especially when challenges arise.

What Matters

"What matters most for parents of gifted/high ability learners?"

Although the answer to this question will differ from one family to another, it's fair to say that it would be whatever is central to, and has a bearing upon, their children's day-to-day well-being.

Let's begin with the fundamentals These include healthy minds and bodies; supports at home and school; physical and emotional safeguards; values; meaningful learning; sense of belonging… And every parent will likely have several other points to add to that list.

However, there are three basic questions that can be helpful when parents consider these fundamentals in relation to their children's well-being:

○ "What can we build upon?"

○ "What needs to change?"

○ "What requires more attention?"

To that end, parents can think about what kinds of guidance, resources, and connectivity are in place. They can share understandings about good physical and mental health. They can appreciate how their kids feel about the various aspects of daily life. They can pay attention to children's actions, reactions, and behaviors as they establish and reach higher goals, invest effort, learn from setbacks, and develop faith in their own abilities. And, in doing this, parents help children bring out and use their best—their strengths, faith, creativity, determination, and enthusiasm.

Questions Parents Often Ask

There are many topics that parents of gifted/high-ability learners want to know more about, and typically these depend upon a constellation of factors pertaining to their own children, family, and life circumstances. Here are four key questions, and answers.

Question 1: "What is the best piece of parenting advice you can offer?"

Respect your child's uniqueness, be attuned to individual needs, and be there to provide love and guidance.

Parents can offer encouragement and support—but a child's destiny is not fully in anyone's control. Parents *cannot*, for example, guarantee their children's mental or physical wellness; that they'll have success in school; that they'll have a supportive circle of friends; that they'll share the same belief system; that they won't experience pain; and that they'll enjoy peace and prosperity through life.

There are, however, many things parents *can* do, and that are within their control. Parents can treat children fairly; show love; provide for their physical needs; give emotional support; help with goal-setting; guide them in decision-making; teach skills and values; demonstrate a solid work ethic; and model appropriate behavior. And, that's a LOT! (For more on these can-do applications, read pp. 5-9 of Sarah Chana Radcliffe's *Raise Your Kids without Raising Your Voice*, and see her *Daily Parenting Posts*.[71]

Question 2: "What are some of the major issues that gifted learners face?"

Sometimes children feel pressure wrestling with a gifted label—or trying to live up to one. They can become too focused on demonstrating or proving their ability, or they may question their self-image. Parents can help kids learn to release the feeling that they have to always "be smart," and appreciate that setbacks are not failures but opportunities for growth. Balancing academic and other demands can be challenging, and children may need assistance with prioritizing, organizing, and finding time to relax and play. Help them revisit expectations, their own and those set by others. Perhaps to-do lists need some revision, clarification or downsizing.

Honor children's capabilities, areas of weakness, interests, and temperament. Encourage them to adjust their efforts to changing demands, environments, and circumstances if need be. Transition times, (such as new classrooms, different programs, shifting social circles, or variable family-related situations) can be difficult. Provide ample opportunity for kids to express concerns or apprehensions, or to request additional help, and be sure to listen carefully to what they have to say. Stay openminded to different ways of solving problems and encouraging children's learning, health, relationships, achievement, and emotional well-being.

Question 3: "My child's interests keep growing and changing all the time. How can I support these?"

It's good for children to want to try new, unique, or challenging activities, including ones they may be hesitant to try. Help them welcome every chance to be free-spirited and imaginative. They can start by building on what they already know, or brainstorming with others, or letting their minds wander and thinking in different and unexpected ways. Parents can recognize previous kids' initiatives and accomplishments—they're stepping stones to new ones.

Research demonstrates that reading, language, music, and movement can improve children's cognitive development, including better developed and coordinated neural networks. Encourage poetry, art, dance, or whatever stimulates the senses. These pursuits can work to activate parts of the brain, and enhanced capacities translate into more efficient learning, as well as more excitement about learning, and more creative expression. Whether interests are technological, intellectual, scientific, athletic, linguistic, cultural, or something else, celebrate spontaneity, curiosity, and playfulness. It's exciting to realize that intelligence changes over time, and that it can be developed with access to rich and fulfilling learning experiences.

Question 4: "How do I know if my child requires testing for gifted education—and what kind of assessment is most suitable?"

The goal of assessment shouldn't be to label children but to inform decision-making about how to meet individual learning needs. Generally speaking, IQ tests make sense when they're used to understand a child's learning problems at a specific point in time, which is what they were designed for. An intelligence test score may provide useful clues about a child's educational needs, but it should be considered alongside additional sources of information such as academic achievement, interest, and persistence—as each of these applies to specific subject areas. Assessments can indicate domains of strength or weakness, and whether a child's abilities are advanced compared to other children the same age.

However, a one-time IQ score is not a predictor of future competence or success. Intelligence is not stable. It changes with motivation, effort, and opportunities to learn. Moreover, tests do not predict adaptability, resilience, or the different kinds of environments a person might be exposed to or the experiences they might have over time. Although a high test-score may meet certain criteria for gifted identification and programing purposes—and indicate excellent test-taking skills and reasoning ability—a child who scores below a designated cut-off may also benefit from gifted programming applications. There are diverse ways of being smart, across academic and non-academic domains. A multiple-measures approach is the best way to identify children's advanced abilities, and to make carefully reasoned decisions about how to meet their ever-changing needs. Good assessment practices are flexible, multi-faceted, fair, and unbiased. They're also aligned with educational practices, meaningful for the individual, and prepare the way for effective learning.

This is an important topic, and it may generate further questions. To find out more, see "Intelligence, IQ, Tests, and Assessments: What Do Parents Need to Know? And What Should They Tell Their Kids" (co-authored with Dona Matthews) in the book *Success Strategies for Parenting Gifted Kids: Expert Advice from the National Association for Gifted Children*. In *Being Smart about Gifted Education*, we discuss identification, testing, and assessment more fully, over the course of three chapters. In *Beyond Intelligence: Secrets for Raising Happily Productive Kids* we have a full chapter entitled "A Parents' Guide to Tests and Assessments." And, as we state (on page 105), "*The best assessment practices are rooted in classroom practice, when teachers take a diagnostic approach and use children's understandings to inform daily instruction.*"

Questions Parents of High-Ability Learners Can Ask Themselves

Here is a list of a dozen important questions for parents to consider. These are not just simple yes/no questions (which would tend to generate simple yes/no answers). Rather, they are "in what ways" questions, designed to help parents think about how they're already being supportive, and what they might want to consider going forward.

1. In what ways do I demonstrate that I am an active and attentive listener?

2. In what ways do I demonstrate resilience, perseverance, and a healthy perspective on the ups and downs of daily life?

3. In what ways do I pay attention to the different factors that could have an impact on my children's cognitive, emotional, social, or behavioral development?

4. In what ways do I try to ensure that my children are appropriately challenged at school?

5. In what ways do I regularly seek information about high-level development?

6. In what ways do I expose my children to experiences that encourage play, exploration, sharing, communication, independence, and learning—in response to their individual abilities, interests, and needs?

7. In what ways do I foster my children's social skills and emotional development?

8. In what ways do I advocate for the most appropriate academic opportunities (ones that suit domain-specific levels of advancement) for my children and others?

9. In what ways do I encourage my children to self-advocate for their own educational needs?

10. In what ways do I collaborate with teachers, consultants, other parents, and members of the community to create robust and engaging learning environments?

11. In what ways do I encourage my children's creative expression?

12. In what ways do I celebrate my children's successes with them?

13. Most importantly, parents can question their own assumptions, inferences, and perceptions. They can also explore how to strengthen their own support networks, how look after themselves better, and how to continue strengthening the parent-child relationship.

Questions Parents of High-Ability Learners Can Ask Their Kids

Martin Luther King said, "*Life's most persistent and urgent question is, "What are you doing for others?"*"

In the spirit of that quote, perhaps the quintessential question any parent can ask children is "How can I help?"

When kids are experiencing difficulty or uncertainties, it can be useful to start moving toward solutions by getting a clearer understanding of what's going. Here are two simple questions to help identify and clarify an issue: "What is the problem?" and "Is it really a problem?" Some children like to tackle challenges and solve issues independently. Other kids appreciate hearing, "How can we work together to make things better?" Parents can be respectful of children's abilities and developing individuality, and yet be supportive, too. All children, no matter how smart they are, need help at some point to deal with the many and inevitable complexities of life. They may require reassurance, or assistance, or encouragement to find ways to manage a situation and to develop the confidence and coping skills they'll need to be resilient in the future.

Albert Einstein said, "*Learn from yesterday, live for today, hope for tomorrow. The important thing is not to stop questioning.*"

R We There Yet? Reflecting upon Parents' and Teachers' Roles

Parents and teachers often share common goals, and thus are well positioned to nurture children's gifted/high-level development by working together to support and enhance learning. Three important points include: 1) **receptivity** to change, 2) **resourcefulness**, and 3) **reassurance**.

Some time ago, I wrote an article about parents' **r**oles and **r**esponsibilities for nurturing gifted learners, and it became the impetus for my ABC series featured in *Parenting for High Potential*. I've **r**evised that piece significantly here but the answer to the title question "Are We There Yet?" was, and still is, "no." I believe we have to thoughtfully implement strategies to **r**everse the tide. **R**ead and **r**eflect: **R** *you* there yet?

Receptivity to Change

Be open-minded, and ready to offer help with children's adjustment to new learning situations or programs.

○ **R**espect—stay attuned to and be respectful of individual differences, learning preferences, interests, and areas of strength and weakness.

○ **R**ecognize—is there exceptional capability in one or more areas, requiring programming adaptations, changes in instructional methods, or differentiated learning experiences?

○ **R**ightness—are educational provisions fitting, meaningful, and timely?

○ **R**eassess—monitor and re-evaluate advancement on an ongoing and targeted basis, to ensure appropriate programming. (See the points "*Assessment*" and "**Above-level testing**" under **A**, and the questions in **Q**.)

○ **R**ange—understand the importance of an array of learning options that vary with respect to depth and scope. What is available in your district?

○ **R**ecommendations—don't rush. Carefully consider the many influences and factors that may have an impact on your child's development. Consider the options. Listen to professionals you trust and who know your child, and then reflect upon what they have to say.

○ **R**eadiness—be mindful that ability develops step by step. A person has to be able to walk before being able to run.

○ **R**eflection—it's about thinking out why things happen the way they do, and how we feel about that. For example, "Why did that occur?" and "What might have happened if I'd done something differently?" Being reflective helps to connect actions with hopes and dreams. This is true for parents as they help children find their way, but it's also true for kids as they learn the value of thinking things through.

○ **R**ealize limitations—accept what a child can and cannot do. But also know when to encourage that child to strive toward easing—or possibly sailing—beyond limits. Poet Louisa May Alcott said, "*I am not afraid of storms for I am learning how to sail my ship.*"

○ **R**esolve—not giving up! A strong problem-solving attitude, a measure of creativity, and a willingness to ask for help when necessary all show resolve. Great for adults as they work to support children's advancement. And, great for kids who seek to meet challenges head on.

○ **R**easonable goals—help children learn to set objectives that are sensible. That is, beneficial, level-headed, and attainable.

○ **R**eview—it's smart for parents to regularly go over various perspectives, processes, recommendations, goals, and decisions. Listen. Think. Read. Learn. Many parents have read *A Parents' Guide to Gifted Children* by James Webb, Janet Gore, Edward Amend, and Arlene Devries. And, over the years, parents and teachers have often referred to NAGC's edited guide book *Parenting Gifted Children*. It contains 54 chapters written by experienced professionals about a sizeable range of topics including assessment, diversity, programming options, family dynamics, advocacy, dual exceptionality, and social and emotional issues.

○ **R**est, **R**ecreation, and **R**elaxation—these three **R**'s are really important for recharging energy and igniting creativity.

○ **R**ealistic—re-calibrate expectations about school changes when they occur. This might apply to programs, teachers, protocols, instructional methods, and so on, within a school or when a child moves to a new school or district. Be patient.

Resourcefulness

Tap into support systems and community resources, and seek information from multiple sources to facilitate children's play, exploration, learning, and development.

○ **R**apport and **R**elationships—a climate of mutual trust is good for everyone. Friendships, family togetherness, mentorships, and different kinds of social interactions help children learn the value of connectivity.

○ **R**isk-taking—actions children take should always be within reason, and with safety in mind. Encourage kids to find a balance between extending frontiers too cautiously and too aggressively. This includes online investigations!

○ **R**elevance—real-world significance makes learning more interesting, and it's a powerful motivator. Kids can create hypotheses; combine logic and vision; examine beliefs and assumptions; seek proof; assess arguments; ask pertinent questions; work toward solving real-world problems; and find other ways to make "authentic learning" a part of their own personal curriculum.

○ **R**esponsibility—facilitate lots of opportunities for children to become responsible for their own actions and their learning, even when it may be challenging. That's how kids succeed. Author Jessica Lahey writes about this in *The Gift of Failure: How the Best Parents Learn to Let Go So Their Children Can Succeed.* Her recommendations (on page 17) include:

"Parenting for autonomy. Parenting for independence and a sense of self born of real competence not misguided confidence. Parenting in the face of failures and setbacks. Parenting for what is right and good in the final tally not for what feels right and good in the moment. Parenting for tomorrow not just for today."

In other words, don't *"parent for dependence"*—parent so kids will become increasingly responsible for themselves.

○ **R**eading—perhaps the most powerful means of learning, and a stimulating and close-at-hand way to find out about the world and all that it has to offer. Kids can read by themselves, but it's also important to read aloud to them. That will help to build their knowledge base, increase their vocabulary, set the tone for life-long reading, and foster connectivity. Make time for reading aloud. (It has even been tagged as a "secret" for raising smarter kids.[72]) For a list of *"Good Books for Bright Kids"* from pre-kindergarten through to young adult, check out the online link provided by Johns Hopkins Center for Talent Development.[73]

○ **R**ecord-keeping—maintain up-to-date information on what's happening in a child's life. Retain a record of activities that illustrate abilities in different areas. It becomes a source of information for purposes of advocacy, and can also be inspirational for children as they continue to build upon their skills or look back upon them later on.

○ **R**epresentation—advocate in constructive ways. Consider joining or creating a network of parents of gifted learners or some other group that will inform and scaffold your efforts, and to which you can contribute meaningfully.

Reassurance

Emphasize that individual differences are normal and accepted, diversity is a strength, and support is available.

○ **R**esilience—not everything comes easily, and children often need help seeing errors as learning opportunities. Sometimes interesting quotes can help them appreciate this. Twenty-five resilience-related quotes for kids are posted in a compilation on the *Roots of Action* website.[74] (Along with some articles for parents, too.)

○ **R**espond—react *kindly* and *attentively* to a child's emotional, social or academic concerns and issues. Consider what kinds of responses resonate most strongly for your children.

○ **R**eaffirm and **R**einforce—stay positive as you continue to encourage a child's personal growth. (See Rebecca Eane's *Positive Parenting* workbook.)

○ **R**iches—nurture the mind, creative expression, and the various social, emotional, cultural, and spiritual dimensions of children's lives. Their individualism in youth is the bedrock for who they will become as they continue to develop their strengths.

○ **R**eality check—encourage children to take time to think about what really matters to them—and why.

○ **R**ally—collaborate, share ideas, and join forces with others from different communities, cultures, networks, and beyond. And rejoice for lots of very good reasons.

S is for Support

I've assembled a selection of sound but simple-to-execute strategies using separate subheadings: 1) ***Supporting Self-confidence and Skill-building***, 2) ***Supporting Schooling***, and 3) ***Supporting Success***. Each section speaks to a specific set of straight-forward suggestions.

Supporting Self-Confidence and Skill-Building

○ **S**eparate—children are not adults. They are very different demographics. Although a child may master a subject like a more mature individual, s/he's still a child.

○ **S**ensitivity—practice it 24-7, especially when dealing with the social-emotional side of giftedness or high-level development. Sometimes kids experience a struggle, for example, during times of transition, or when having difficulty trying to fit in. By being patient, sensitive to their feelings, and understanding of their behaviors, adults can help them to feel supported and soothed.

○ **S**oothe—calm the spirit while educating the mind so both work in harmony. In *Parenting with Presence: Practices for Raising Conscious, Confident, Caring Kids*, author Susan Stiffelman writes about how to turn parenting into more of a spiritual practice by means of awareness, and by bringing peace, joy, and greater consciousness into family life and child-rearing approaches. She discusses communication, empathy, relationships, and more.

○ **S**pace—make sure children have plenty of downtime, including times and places to relax and daydream. Kids also need workspaces for schoolwork, and to be able to pursue creative outlets. Such spaces may be quiet and private, or more bustling. Preferences and requirements may change depending on the activity and degree of focus.

○ **S**afe—assure children that whatever they think, it's safe to express their thoughts and opinions with you. A safe environment is one wherein children can explore their feelings, try out different ways of learning, be creative, and advance comfortably. Safety is a defining element for any child's optimal growth and well-being.

○ **S**tretch—encourage kids to expand their comfort zones, and to try something they've never done before, whether they think they'll be good at it or not. (See the "Stretching" segment under the letter "**B**" in this book.)

○ **S**elf-assessment—when children become aware of the connections they are making between what they already know and what they are learning, they become better able to monitor their own progress, and to ascertain where they might need to work harder to get to the next level.

○ **S**potlight—many strengths and successes lie outside the academic realm, in activities such as volunteering, singing in a choir, learning synchronized swimming, puppetry, or karate. Encourage your child to become involved in different kinds of activities, and to share these times with friends.

○ **S**urround—encourage play and connectivity with a wide circle of children, not just academic peers.

○ **S**ignals—watch for signs that your child may be ready to tackle something more interesting or challenging. Or possibly something that's more fun, less taxing, more physically oriented, or a departure from everyday kinds of pursuits.

Supporting Schooling

○ **S**hare—chat with other parents about what does and does not work as you move through the gifted education maze.

○ **S**trengthen—strive to fortify the bonds between home and school so children know that the adults in their lives are working cohesively together in their best interest.

○ **S**earch—keep looking for the right options to keep your child motivated to learn. For example, possibilities might include acceleration, differentiation, ability grouping, and project-based activities. For extensive resources on a broad range of gifted-related topics such as testing, schools, programs, supportive websites, books, associations, twice-exceptional learners, and social-emotional development, check out the database at the Davidson Institute.[75]

○ **S**ynthesize—sometimes homework seems fractured. Try weaving the thematic threads together to help your child see the Big Picture.

○ **S**pearhead—if your school district has a parent support group for gifted education, join it. If not, organize one. There's power in numbers.

○ **S**implify—you can't change the entire system in a single semester or school year. Prioritize. Decide what's really important, and work on that first.

○ **S**chool—make the broader world your child's classroom, whether it's the grocery or hardware store, or the neighborhood skating rink or waterpark. There's an old saying, *"A child educated only in school is an uneducated child."*

○ **S**kill—what special skill can you offer at your child's school? Perhaps you could start a student newspaper or an art club or inspire kids by sharing interesting information about your work or hobbies. Or maybe you know of a family member or good friend who has expertise in a specific area and who would be willing to share some of their knowledge with kids?

○ **S**tudy—be prepared with facts, figures, and a possible plan of action before complaining that your child's needs are not being met.

○ **S**ensible—no-one likes a ranting, raging, red-in-the-face parent, so be sensible in your dealings with teachers and administrators. (See the next chapter for tips for working with teachers.)

○ **S**ounding board—be gracious and willing to listen to the parents of other or younger gifted learners who may seek your ear, advice, and recommendations. You may also learn something valuable from them.

Supporting Success!

○ **S**avor—enjoy the uniqueness of your child's giftedness, whatever challenges it presents.

○ **S**timulate—most machines wear out from rust, not over-use. So it is with the brain!

○ **S**ideline—set aside wanting to live through your child's accomplishments. Whatever you're pushing for should be in his or her best interest, not yours, or your ego's.

○ **S**how up—even if you don't understand robotics or you hate chess—be there when your child wants your input, needs your support, or exhibits a special interest or talent.

○ **S**ureness—don't be so sure that you know what's best in every situation. Open your mind and your heart to new ideas from various sources.

○ **S**pirited—some children may seem "difficult"—or irritable or demanding or fussy. Triggers may include transitions, distractions, new situations, self-doubt, or challenges. And some kids have a temperament that predisposes them toward certain kinds of behaviors. Parents can support children who are spirited by remaining focused on their positive attributes, and by encouraging these. For more on this particular topic, see Dona Matthews' articles and suggested resources in her column "Going Beyond Intelligence."[76]

○ **S**peak up—when you have an opinion, concern, or good suggestion, respectfully let others know. Don't assume that they can read your mind.

○ **S**ojourn—the journey of helping children reach their potential can be a very long and arduous road. It can also be intriguing, exciting, and gratifying. Appreciate the scenery when you reach a pleasant spot along the way.

○ **S**mile—lighten up. You can accomplish a lot more with a smile than with a scowl or a furrowed brow.

○ **S**alute—you deserve one for advocating strongly and suitably.

Supplementary **S**hout-out: **S**everal years ago, *Parenting for High Potential* reader Judie Becker from Kansas **s**ent me **s**everal **s**elf-**s**elected and **s**plendid **s**uggestions for **s**upporting giftedness. I've included most of her ideas here. Thanks, Judie!

T is for Tips for Working with Teachers

For parents of toddlers to teens, here are some treasured and time-tested tips. **Thoughts** about working with **teachers** are followed by: 1) *Traits to Tap*, 2) *Top-notch Things to Try*, and 3) *Tactics for Turbulence and Transition Times*.

Thoughts about Teachers: What Matters

The ideal learning environment is safe and welcoming. Creativity abounds, and children are happy and motivated. Their individual learning needs are met, intelligence-building is a priority, and the teacher is a caring, skilled professional.

Does this sound like your child's classroom? Think about it, and hopefully, the answer is yes. If the answer is no—or maybe—then perhaps it's a compelling reason to think even harder about what's going on, and how to support teachers.

By understanding and appreciating educators' work, parents are better able to forge meaningful partnerships with them, leading toward more positive outcomes for kids. Teachers have a broad range of tools, skills, resources, networks, and supports that parents may not see or fully appreciate. Teachers plan lessons, prepare instruction, collaborate with others, attend professional development sessions, and seek new ways to motivate students. Teachers differentiate programs, set appropriate expectations, study curriculum guidelines, monitor students' efforts, offer guidance and assistance, assess progress, write reports, and juggle all kinds of administrative responsibilities. Teachers demonstrate and teach virtues such as kindness, honesty, respect, integrity, and fairness because children learn from what they see, hear, and experience. Teachers listen, encourage, console, and reinforce, and they reflect upon their own practice. Teachers promote inquiry and playful exploration in the classroom, and beyond.

Teaching is not just a job—it's a calling. Granted, not all teachers are stellar in every way. Like the rest of us, they have areas of strength and weakness, and failings from which they can learn to become more competent.

Four teachers have written a chapter entitled "Pathways to Supporting the Gifted: Four Educators' Personal Journeys" within the book *Nurturing the Development of GATE Teachers*. The chapter's co-authors, Barbara Ruf, Stephen Shroeder-Davis, Jane Hesslein, and William Keilty each describe what it was like being a young gifted learner, and how they later became educators in gifted programs. They share insightful views of what they have learned over the years. They write that common precursors in their experience of becoming teachers included "*lifelong curiosity, self-direction, and boldness and creativity in the generation of new ideas and solutions.*" They go on to suggest that, "*Just as gifted students vary in their abilities and needs, the ability to react to those needs requires flexibility, independence, courage, and creativity.*"

Excellent suggestions! However, the reality is, that not all teachers have these capacities. Teacher training and professional development focusing on gifted-related learning requirements should be an ongoing part of every educator's learning curve. This includes content that will help teachers learn to refine materials, instruction, assessment methods, goals, and other ways to better support and encourage children's high-level development, and also their diverse social, emotional, motivational, and other needs. If every school and district had robust cadres of teachers who were well-trained in gifted education, there would be a stronger educational system all around. After all, being an educator is about teaching *and* learning.

The best teachers are actively engaged in their own personal growth, including making time for family, friends, and colleagues, and for developing their own intelligences and creativity. They demonstrate the importance of all of this. The best teachers hone their skills, challenging themselves to become more effective day after day, and year after year—and they take pride in their work. But that work is not easy, and they cannot do it alone.

Parents who appreciate this will step up to help build effective partnerships with their child's teachers. By understanding what teachers do, and how they go about doing it, parents are better equipped to b effective collaborators and advocates for children's learning.

Here are traits to tap, things to try, and tactics to help teachers in the course of their work, and when kids encounter problems or face times of transition.

Traits to Tap

When meeting with teachers to strengthen home and school connections or to resolve issues, it's best to be as open and positive as possible.

Be:

○ **T**hankful—convey gratitude for the work teachers do.

○ **T**horough—do your "homework" and get the facts straight before confronting the teacher about issues having to do with your child.

○ **T**houghtful—give preliminary thought to what *you* think might work to ameliorate any specific difficulties, and also how to build bridges with the school. Listen thoughtfully to the teachers' ideas and responses to your questions and suggestions. It might be beneficial to take notes. This could help to ensure that you have a clear sense of the conversation, plus you will be able to reflect upon the notes later.

○ **T**ruthful—be honest about any concerns you might have, and why they matter.

○ **T**ough—maintain resolve but do so while being mindful of the perspectives of others.

○ **T**imely—be considerate of people's busy schedules. Strive to find convenient, appropriate times for conversations with the teacher about what you (or perhaps they) think requires address.

○ **T**actful—watch your tone, written communication, words, facial expressions, gestures, and body language, all of which convey messages and reveal attitudes and undertones.

○ **T**ranquil—adopt a calm, diplomatic approach that will help drive momentum forward. Tension is counterproductive.

Things to Try

Teachers typically have a "toolbox" of top strategies that they use to make classrooms welcoming, effective learning environments. Here are tips for parents who want to fortify the contents of any such toolbox.

Add:

○ **T**rust—let teachers, counselors, and school administrators know that you have confidence in them, and in everyone's ability to work collaboratively. Perhaps you can point to one or two examples of this. Confidence is empowering!

○ **T**eamwork—bring your strengths and viewpoints to the table. Tie them constructively to others' contributions, coordinate efforts, and thereby develop a shared ethic.

○ **T**railblazing—be creative. Think in new and innovative ways.

○ **T**racking—keep track of your child's accomplishments so teachers can build upon what you know about your child. Tip: don't bring entire videos, photo albums, or scrapbooks. A few succinct but carefully selected descriptors or examples will do.)

○ **T**alk—facilitate dialogue. Clarify, discuss, and extend ideas. Engage in "self-talk" as well—that is, an inner dialogue that facilitates a thoughtful clarification and review of a situation before, during, and after taking action.

○ **T**raining—advocate for additional teacher training opportunities. For instance, professional development on differentiating programming for gifted/high-ability learners, or workshops on promoting inquiry-based learning, or learning sessions on incorporating multicultural

considerations into gifted educational offerings, or more gifted certifi-
cation courses, or...

○ **T**asks—suggest ideas for activities and learning experiences that relate
to your child's particular interests, including those in non-curricular
areas. Tasks don't necessarily have to be work-oriented, or big. Helen
Keller said, "*I long to accomplish great and noble tasks, but it is my chief
duty to accomplish small tasks as if they were great and noble.*" There's
gratification from accomplishment.

○ **T**hinking skills—help children develop their creative and critical
thinking skills. Thinking underlies the basic elements of every-day life:
speaking, listening, reading, and writing. It propels learning and advancement. Low-order thinking skills include remembering, comprehending,
and actively listening and processing information. High-order thinking
skills include intricately questioning, interpreting, constructing, and
then evaluating new knowledge. Higher mental processes depend on
social interactions (such as play and collaboration), and also on development in different cognitive domains. This involves maturity, but also
experiences such as finding and using information, and being able to
adapt to and interact with the environment. There are exciting programs
for developing thinking skills online and elsewhere. For a practical start,
children and teens can check out Hoagies' Gifted Education Page for
Kids.[77] And, for adults, there are interesting thinking skills strategies
offered online in articles posted by the Davidson Institute.[78]

○ **T**echnology—find out what's of-the-moment, and how it can enhance
learning and teaching at home and at school. There are (literally) bil-
lions of web pages, and loads of resources and educational offerings
including programs, lessons, online programs, and on and on and on,
in every domain. Be selective.[79] Have a look at Joanne Orlando's blog
for information and advice on how to keep technology use safe, how
to navigate today's increasingly "digital lifestyle," and how to manage
problems that might arise. She is an expert on "*educational, ethical, and
social issues that arise from our technology use.*"[80] (See also "**C**omputer
and electronic devices," and "**O**nline" points within this book).

○ **T**alent development—the University of Connecticut is home to the Renzulli Center for Gifted Education, Creativity, and Talent Development.[81] Under its heading "Resources and Services" there's an extensive list of websites to tap, including information indexes, search engines, student research resources, web portals, libraries and museums, and so forth. Another solid place to acquire information on giftedness and talent development is the Belin-Blank Center, which is part of the College of Education at the University of Iowa. Their mission is "*to empower and serve the international gifted community through exemplary leadership in programs, research, and advocacy.*"[82] And, the Center for Talent Development at Northwestern University offers "*programs and resources for academically talented students, their families and educators*"— and has done so for over three decades.[83]

Turbulence and Transition Times

Sometimes problems arise, requiring parents and teachers to strategically focus on improving the status quo for a child. The approach will depend on circumstances, but here are some tactical measures to consider.

Prepare to:

○ **T**rouble-shoot—help to determine the source or causes of a problem. Sometimes what underlies a problem is temporary, tangential, or simple to address. Sometimes it's more complex. Work through the underlying aspects of whatever is problematic in order to decide if it's truly worth pursuing or whether the matter might resolve on its own accord.

○ **T**olerate—show patience, and a willingness to chat, weigh alternatives, and possibly compromise. Avoid coming across as unyielding, confrontational, short-tempered or disrespectful.

○ **T**weak—don't attempt to fix everything all at once. Take it one bit at a time.

○ **T**wist, **T**urn, **T**ry—be amenable to looking in alternative directions, such as consulting with different people, considering different resolutions, and exploring ideas from different contexts or viewpoints.

○ **T**read carefully—be part of the solution, not part of the problem.

○ **T**arget—find out what's really at issue, what's already been done to ameliorate it, and what you can do to help today, tomorrow, and beyond.

○ **T**riumph—remember that when troublesome situations occur, parents, teachers, and children can work *together* toward transforming turmoil into a triumphant tour de force.

U is for Understanding

There's no **u**ltimate, **u**tterly **u**nflawed, or **u**niversal approach for supporting gifted/high-ability learners. **U**nquestionably, however, there are **u**seful guidelines to help parents think intelligently and sensitively about how to proceed. Don't **u**nderestimate the **u**nderlying value of these **u**ndeniably **u**n-ignorable suggestions.

○ **U**nderstanding—find out all you can about giftedness, including its conceptual base, its implications, its joys, and its complexities.

○ **U**ncover—carefully sift through reputable sources of information about gifted learners and approaches to gifted education. Thoughtfully consider the material, and the various and sometimes conflicting perspectives. However, be mindful of what's best for your own child and family dynamic.

○ **U**niqueness—appreciate that giftedness is an individual differences phenomenon. There's an abundance of support services that can help parents address children's unique gifts and talents, and also provide resources. Many have already been mentioned throughout the course of this book. However, the Institute for Educational Advancement is one more avenue to explore. The IEA is a non-profit organization that has served "*highly able, creative children ages 2-18*" for the past 20 years, offering programs, consulting, and resources to families, schools, and districts—including labs, support groups, information about advocacy, and assistance with twice-exceptional learners. IEA provides "*customized programs that match individuals' unique gifts and talents with the most appropriate mentors, schools, and other learning resources to maximize each student's intellectual and personal development.*"[84]

○ **U**ncertainty—there's a lot we have yet to learn about high-level development. Children can experience bouts of uncertainty about themselves, about their place in the ever-changing world, and about what they can and cannot achieve. As a result, they may be unhappy, or unsure how or even if to advance. Offer reassurance and respond to their questions and concerns.

○ **U**nderachievement—this can be problematic because not all smart kids extend themselves or achieve what they're capable of achieving. There are many possible reasons for that, such as poor work habits, inappropriate instruction, under or overly challenging programming, stress, disabilities, pressure at home or elsewhere, and other circumstances that can affect productivity and the enjoyment of learning. The best ways to address underachievement will depend on the specific reasons for it. For example, a child might benefit from stronger role models, more realistic expectations, or more or less independence or structure. If underperformance is a concern, have a look at the relevant literature. One option is *Why Bright Kids Get Poor Grades and What You Can Do about It* by Sylvia Rimm, and another is Todd Stanley's book *When Smart Kids Underachieve at School: Practical Solutions for Teachers*. (The latter informs educators but it's an enlightening read for parents, too).

○ **U**pbeat—attitude matters. Accentuate the positive. Indeed, psychology teaches us that positivity has a beneficial impact on creativity, knowledge acquisition, play, courage, resilience, relationships, and other lived experiences, and helps to make them more meaningful. For more on this, see the book *Ungifted: Intelligence Redefined* by Scott Barry Kaufman. (Coincidentally, it starts with the letter **U**!)

○ **U**neven development—accept that developmental pathways are diverse, and that developmental asynchrony is not uncommon.

○ **U**nconditional love—know that this is a given. Never compromised.

○ **U**pset—there's no point in getting uptight, uppity, or upset when others have difficulty understanding what giftedness is about. Misconceptions abound, and yes, they can be unsettling. However, chatting with people about their assumptions or mistaken beliefs, and being respectfully informative about the "g word" can help smooth the way.

○ **U**ntrained teachers—advocate for more teacher preparation, training, and professional growth programs that will enable educators to be increasingly competent and targeted in their work with gifted learners.[85] As I write elsewhere,

"When teachers are offered and choose to avail themselves of opportunities to think constructively about giftedness and issues pertaining to high-level development, and to develop sound approaches for working with exceptional learners—and when they are administratively supported in this regard—the system and everyone in it stands to benefit."[86]

○ **U**nusual circumstances—recognize that each learning environment, set of circumstances, social milieu, transition, educational decision, span of growing up years, and opportunity for authentic self-discovery has its very own stamp of distinction—to be reflected upon, and addressed accordingly.

○ **U**nstructured time—learning often occurs unexpectedly, when kids are playing or just having fun with family or friends. Routines, timelines, and schedules can be beneficial, but always having to adhere to them can make life pretty humdrum. Some kids prefer orderliness and consistency. Yet there should also be plenty of room for spontaneity and unstructured downtime.

○ **U**nplug—kids who are constantly connected to an electronic device miss out on opportunities to connect with people.

○ **U**nwavering—provide support, encouragement, and guidance on an ongoing basis.

○ **U**nlimited—there's no end to what gifted learners can accomplish with the right opportunities and supports!

○ **U**nequivocal—acknowledge and stand up for the irrefutable right for appropriate, meaningful educational experiences for *all* children.

V is for Viewpoints

Parents have varying *viewpoints* on how to encourage children's high-level development. Voila! Here are fifteen **VIPs**—*Very Important Perspectives*—for parents to consider. I invite you to prioritize this list for yourself because then you'll be thinking even more carefully about the points!

○ **V**alues—integrity, honesty, respect, compassion… What's on your list of virtues that children should learn, and that cannot be compromised?

○ **V**erification—help children find truth, relevance, and meaning in what they undertake to accomplish. It will spark their interest and motivation.

○ **V**oice—kids have to be able to express their opinions, concerns, and ideas—and possibly even vent. That means parents have to listen attentively in order to respond.

○ **V**enture—explore, discover, play. These are all action verbs that pave the way for learning and personal growth from infancy right through adulthood.

○ **V**enue—the dictionary defines venue as "a place of action." It might be a home, a school, a store, a park, a beach, a forest, a museum, a gallery or anywhere children can acquire varied experience of the vast world around them. The more venues visited, the more vistas, and vantage points.

○ **V**ision—and, following that thought about venues, the more kids *see*, the more they learn.

○ **V**olition—the act of choosing whether to put forth effort, be creative, engage in activities, collaborate with others—these are just some of the many choices that affect children's well-being and achievement levels. Kids have to be *willing* to try, and to learn from their mistakes.

○ **V**ersatility—children may want to pursue a variety of whims and interests, and why not? However, they might need support switching from one area of focus to another. And, they likely won't be equally adept at everything they try. Be available to offer guidance and encouragement when kids' inclinations vacillate or veer.

○ **V**icissitudes—life is full of ups and downs. Nothing is really certain, and goals can be hard won, so children have to learn about resilience and a growth mindset. For more information on this, see the article "Mindsets and Gifted Education: Transformation in Progress."[87] Also, Jacqui LeTran is a self-described "mindset mentor" who focuses on inner strengths, including how to use the mind to control and bolster words, body, imagination, courage, forgiveness, love, and perseverance—and thereby gain the self-confidence needed to deal with the vicissitudes of life. Her book *Unleash Your Inner Super Powers,* and her work (primarily with teens), offer insight for people of all ages.[88]

○ **V**igor—children who demonstrate vitality, vivaciousness, and vehemence, including strength of character, strength of convictions, and strength in various areas, are forces to be reckoned with. Very positive forces.

○ **V**olunteerism—it's imperative that we show children how they can contribute to the community. Continue to reinforce children's commitment to the greater good.

○ **V**anguard—it means being at the forefront of a movement. Is your child a leader or a follower? Being on the frontline takes grit. For more on this, see *Grit: The Power of Passion and Perseverance* by Angela Duckworth.

○ **V**ictory!—success comes in different guises, and there is no one measure of it. How do you gauge success? More importantly perhaps, how does your child? Maybe success comes from knowing oneself and becoming the best person possible. Or perhaps contentment and productivity are determiners of success. Winston Churchill said, *"Success is not final, failure is not fatal. It is the courage to continue that counts."* Could valor be the magic elixir?

○ **V**ulnerability—the most capable children are also capable of being troubled or hurt. They may also have difficulty academically or socially. Parents can give them strategies to stay safe and confident, and share their own experiences of overcoming challenges and adversity.

○ **V**igilance—in the whole scheme of things, it's smart for parents to be watchful and wise. But *wait*—that's the letter **W**. Next up…

W is for Wondering and Well-being

Socrates said, *"Wisdom begins in wonder."* That is as true now as it ever **was**.

In this segment I **write** about *wondering*—that is, the many **what**, **when**, and **why** questions gifted learners have; **where** they can go for answers; how they can thrive; and **who** they may become as they develop their capabilities.

A while ago I **wrote** a poem **wherein** I revealed the **wistful, weighty, wishful,** and occasionally **worried words** of children **wrestling** with a **whirl** of questions about giftedness. I share those **written words wholeheartedly.**

Together, let's continue to seek the best possible answers to all these questions children have about their ***well-being***.

"They Tell Me I'm Gifted..."

They tell me I'm gifted… What does this mean?
Is this something new, or have I always been?

> *They tell me I'm gifted… I'm not quite sure why.*
> *But everyone thinks my "potential" is high.*

They tell me I'm gifted… With increased understanding.
I wonder—will this make my life more demanding?

> *They tell me I'm gifted… Although I'm not sure*
> *If it's something I'm meant to enjoy or endure.*

They tell me I'm gifted… It must be for real.
But it doesn't explain all the things that I feel.

They tell me I'm gifted… I wish I were wise
'Cause then I might know what the label implies.

They tell me I'm gifted… And if this is true
Does this signify I have more "gifts" than you?

They tell me I'm gifted… Who really knows?
Is it something unseen, or something that shows?

They tell me I'm gifted… Can this be outgrown?
What's in my future? It's all so unknown!

They tell me I'm gifted… Yet they don't explain
*If it's **all** of me, or just a part of my brain.*

They tell me I'm gifted… Is that a fact?
Do I have to change how I think, feel, and act?

They tell me I'm gifted… From whose point of view?
Does this mean that I am no longer like you?

They tell me I'm gifted… Could this be a blessing?
Who knows for sure, and who's only guessing?

They tell me I'm gifted… What should I do now?
Do I shrug? Do I laugh? Do I cry? Do I bow?

They tell me I'm gifted… They say I'm unique.
Do I have to show strengths? Can't I ever be weak?

They tell me I'm gifted… Now I'm in a jam.
Do they think I'm smarter than I really am?

They tell me I'm gifted… Is it destiny?
Controlled by what's inside or outside of me?

They tell me I'm gifted… I think that means able.
I hope others know they should look past the label.

They tell me I'm gifted… What do I need?
Love and support that will help me succeed.

They tell me I'm gifted… And so it must be,
But I know deep inside that I'm still only me…

"*They Tell Me I'm Gifted…*" also appears in *Being Smart about Gifted Education, 2nd Edition* (pp. 357-359)

X is for Xtending the Gifted Xperience

Throughout this book, I've shared ideas for offering support, guidance, and encouragement to children and teens as they strive toward success and fulfillment, now **and into the future**. This last point is a critical perspective because gifted learners are, in fact learners across the entire life span! The focus of this chapter is on the **x**perience of giftedness as it **x**tends into adulthood.

Please **x**cuse the **x**change of "e**X**" to "**X**" as I **x**plore ideas here. This **x**ception is **x**plicably due to **x**traordinary circumstances because **X** words are practically **x**tinct!

Xperience: What Matters

A person's xperiences provide context and structure for understanding abilities, preferences, passions, and challenges. Being receptive and proactive, and also trying new xperiences, enables people to realize more fully their intellectual, creative, and emotional abilities. The more we do, the more we learn.

This is true, no matter what someone's age might be. We are never too old to learn! Regardless of whether an xperience relates to social, academic, spiritual, cultural, or other dimensions of someone's life, it opens the door to opportunity and accomplishment. And, potentially, to difficulties which may require redirection of energy, or reconsideration of action plans. (But that becomes another xperience that provides a learning curve.)

Xperience is a teacher. It helps enrich the mind and strengthen the soul. Albert Einstein said, "*The only source of knowledge is xperience.*" And, Eleanor Roosevelt cautioned that, "*People grow through xperience if they meet life honestly and courageously. This is how character is built.*" Countless moment-by-moment occurrences and influences comprise a person's real xperience of life and the world, helping to define who they are, and how they will develop over the course of time. As children grow, they are actively involved in creating their own intelligence, responding to and engaging in autonomous, shared, and multi-sensory learning xperiences, and thereby becoming stronger, wiser, and more self-reliant through to adulthood.

Xperience is also an adventure of sorts. It is unique to the individual and, like life, it is unscripted. Costs, risks, and unknowns can make xperiential learning a bit scary, and that in turn can help children develop tenacity, confidence, judgment, courage, and convictions. That's good. All this helps to build character and, too, is part of the complex journey of maturing.

Xperience is unavoidable. It evolves, and transpires morning, noon, and night whether we are aware of it or not, from cradle to crypt. Helping children to make the most of their lived xperiences over the years—and to find fulfillment in them—is one of the most important responsibilities a parent will ever have. And, when kids become adults, they can, in turn, draw upon their acquired strengths and share those with their own children.

Which brings us full circle, because adults who are gifted learners should not diminish or take their strengths for granted but rather, must always continue to build upon them. Too often, parents are so focused on their children and on managing day to day realities that they do not nurture their own giftedness. That is counterproductive. It's like revving up a car and then letting it sit in the driveway for years. Moreover, children learn best when following the xemplary behavior of adults who value and demonstrate the power of nurturing the mind and body—that is, the intellect as well as the many other dimensions that comprise well-being and self-fulfillment. And, that, in short, is the crux of xperience!

An xcellent book on the gifted xperience as it xtends over the course of people's lives is *The Development of Giftedness and Talent across the Life Span*. Edited by Frances Degen Horowitz, Rena Subotnik, and Dona Matthews, it is a thorough compilation of material contributed by developmental psychologists and xperts in gifted education who discuss giftedness and talent development in different domains, from childhood through later adulthood. Topics include individual differences, high-level abilities, educational practices, and how to promote and sustain the development of giftedness over the years. The authors focus on children *and* adults.

In *Bright Adults: Uniqueness and Belonging across the Life Span*, Ellen Fiedler describes stages of gifted development, referring to "voyagers" (young adults), "navigators" (middle-age adults), and "cruisers" (seniors), and she provides understandings and strategies for enhancing life's journey. And, in Paula Prober's *Your Rainforest Mind: A Guide to the Well-being of Gifted Adults and Youth*, the author suggests that people are like complex ecosystems. She xplains that the term "rainforest mind" refers not only to one's thinking, cognition, and brain functioning but also to the heart, soul, body, and spirit; and she gives strategies to help individuals flourish. Some readers enjoy books that reveal and xtend metaphorical parallels like these (about sailing ships and tropical environments). For anyone seeking a happier and healthier adulthood, there are *many* ways to think of—and also to steer, nurture, and sustain—giftedness, skill-building capacities, and intelligences.

In psychological terms, we can distinguish between fluid intelligence, as might be evidenced by tests of reasoning or pattern detection, and crystallized intelligence, as might be evidenced by measures of general knowledge and vocabulary. But domain-specific xpertise is something yet again. Middle-to-late-year adults who continue to develop knowledge in various and specific domains do themselves a huge favor because they learn more. Plus, by being purposeful, they also help to safeguard their cognitive abilities. Psychologist Scott Barry Kaufman writes that cognitive functions peak at different times, and that instead of looking at adult intelligence *"through the lens of youthful general processing speed and reasoning"* it's better to look at it *"through the lens of xpertise, wisdom, and purpose."*[89]

How, then, can adults make the most of their intelligence and their own xperiential possibilities? Here are some xamples of how they (and their kids) can xtend themselves. (Case in point, notice my xtensive use of **X** words—over 50!—in the following suggestions...)

○ **X**ceptionality—having xtremely advanced ability in one or more areas is a gift, but it requires work if it's going to endure or be maximized. Those who are remiss about fortifying what's already strong run the risk of diminishing it. Some abilities may be off the charts, and others may be less so. Regardless, horizons can be xpansive provided people xercise curiosity, creativity, and critical thinking skills, and are willing to challenge the status quo.

○ **X**pert—you don't have to be the "best of the best" to feel accomplished. Skillfulness is fine, proficiency is good, and mastery is better—but gaining knowledge in and of itself, is always useful.

○ **X**ecute—gaining that aforementioned knowledge is a process, and people have to initiate, engage, and then see things through over time. It's not enough just to have a plan. The doing (or xecution) is what brings it to fruition.

○ **X**ternal influences—distractions can negatively affect or pull people away from achieving their goals. Pay heed to the xtrinsic influences (and influencers) that are positive and motivational, and steer clear of those that xude negativity or compromise intent.

○ **X**cuses—sometimes individuals withdraw, xtricate, or xempt themselves from trying something because it may seem risky, xhausting, difficult, xacting, or unappealing. There's no surer way to squander worthwhile learning xperiences than by refusing to be involved.

○ **X**pediciousness (the "quality of xpediency")—there are many ways to advance. Quickly, slowly, directly, circuitously, bit by bit, or in swoops. Webster's Dictionary equates xpediciousness with "advantageousness" and "advisability." Some people like to rush, but keep in mind that xpedient outcomes can also come by way of a steady, measured approach.

○ **X**aggeration—people who convey an xalted opinion of themselves may seem conceited. (And may also be mistaken about their competencies.) On the other hand, those who xtol their virtues may be confident, have lots of xtra xperience, and might be inclined to work harder to meet self-imposed xpectations. Strive toward xcellence, not arrogance or xcess.

○ **X**travagance—No! Learning xperiences don't have to be xhorbitant, xotic, or xclusive. But they should be meaningful. Therefore, be resourceful! There are unlimited possibilities for enrichment, xcursions, investigations, xperimentation, and pursuit—with options for babies, generation X-ers, seniors, and all those in between.

○ **X**posure—ensure abundant opportunities to play and relax, as well as to learn. As xplained above, these don't have to be xpensive! For xample, check out the gatherings at various local and regional centers. Have a look at the article "Discovering the Gifted Ex-Child" by Stephanie Tolan. It's a time-honored, easily accessible, and relevant resource.[90] Additional material relating to adult giftedness can be found through SENG (Supporting Emotional Needs of the Gifted).[91]

○ **X**uberance—the word is derived from the root "uber" which means to be fruitful. Welcome prospects, xploits, and opportunities to be fruitful wherever you go.

○ **X**tenuating circumstances—life is unpredictable and complicated. We all have to xpect the unexpected. By continuing to develop coping mechanisms and resilience, people learn to mitigate difficulties, and can achieve more success.

○ **X**ecutive functioning—this term refers to a part of the brain that addresses working memory, flexible thinking, and self-control, and it is responsible for such functions as planning, prioritizing, xamining, formulating concepts, regulating emotions, and staying focused. Parents and teachers work with children to support these kinds of skills. Adults should continue to reinforce these functions as well. Brain health should be a priority for *everyone* as they age. (Baycrest is a renowned facility that houses the Centre for Aging and Brain Health Innovation (CABHI).[92] There are helpful resources, including information on research and innovations, accessible online through other areas at Baycrest.[93]

○ **X**ertion—research shows that effort, determination, and xercise help people stay healthy. Commit to energizing the brain, the body, and the spirit—whatever moves you (literally)—and preferably on a regular basis, and on into the later years. It will be xhilarating!

○ **X**citement—a lively, xultant, and fiery approach can turn a task or activity into a burst or xplosion of pleasure. Use joy to advantage to build momentum for learning, doing, and thinking.

○ **X**pression—thoughts and ideas are potentially rich and empowering, albeit sometimes concealed. Each person chooses what to cultivate, reveal, share, or convey, be it through words, art, music, dance, or even silence. So, be careful not to make assumptions about the capabilities of others, or for that matter, yourself. Remember, what people show, communicate, or do is not necessarily reflective of all they're capable of, or all they know.

○ **X**hibit—employ and demonstrate solid work habits, persistence, and a longing to succeed. Achievement and happiness are not givens. They are acquired by means of practice, and perseverance.

○ **X**change—over the years we trade youth for xperience, acquiring wisdom along the way.

○ **X**ploration—elsewhere in this book (xcerpted from **E/X**ploration) are these words: *"Learning is a multi-tiered investigative process, fueled by inspiration, anchored by determination, and enhanced by discovery—from infancy onward."* The *onward* refers, in large part, to adulthood through to old age. Xploration on our own or with others leads to adventure, fun, and breakthroughs, and helps to keep us young.

Y, Z is for Youthful Zeal

> And so, we've reached the end of the alphabet. The focus here is on forward momentum: 1) *yearning*, and 2) *zooming* ahead.

Yearning: What Matters

In order for kids to succeed, they have to try. Moreover, they have to *want* to try. That urge or will, when coupled with the belief that they can prevail, has carried many young people forward toward successful outcomes. Aspirations are great starting points, but it's preparation, hard work, self-discipline, and yearning that rule the day and turn possibilities into accomplishments.

Yearning (Driving force)

○ **Yet**—this is a powerful little word that indicates there's room and impetus to grow. Its open-endedness implies that people can still accomplish things, if they choose to do so. The word "yet" holds promise and optimism.

○ **Yield**—this is also a powerful word because it's indicative of the willingness to show flexibility. Being gracious and amenable to change, even when situations are taxing, are signs of strength and personal growth.

○ **Yes!**—negativity is disheartening, whereas a cheery, hopeful outlook can help lighten the load and motivate children. In *The Yes Brain: How to Cultivate Courage, Curiosity, and Resilience in Your Child*, authors Daniel Siegel and Tina Bryson explain why and also how to help kids develop a "Yes Brain" mindset. They write,

"*When kids work from a* Yes Brain *mentality they are more flexible, open to compromise, more willing to take chances and explore. They're more curious and imaginative, less worried about making mistakes. They're also less rigid and stubborn, which makes them better at relationships and more adaptable and resilient when it comes to handling adversity... They do more, learn more, and become more."*

What parent wouldn't say "*Yes!*" to that?

❍ **Y**awn—it's okay for kids to experience boredom. It's a chance for them to think about what they might want to learn more about, or want to initiate.

❍ **Y**esterdays—the future is dependent on the past. We don't know what lies ahead, but what comes before provides know-how and incentive for our tomorrows.

❍ **Y**outh empowerment—there are humanitarian, social, environmental, and other causes that many children and teens feel strongly about and want to support. In order to be leaders, activists, and change-makers, kids have to have vision, a work ethic, and connectivity with others who share their desire to make a difference. The WE movement is a charity started by two teenage brothers 20 years ago, and it is just one example of an impactful organization that continues to inspire millions of children, families, school communities, and people around the world.[94] Parents can help kids find their passions and also discover ways to participate in efforts to improve the status quo in their home towns or further afield. See Marilyn Price-Mitchell's book *Tomorrow's Change-makers: Reclaiming the Power of Citizenship for a New Generation.*

❍ **Y**oung children—how children learn, and how to support them in that has been the overarching focus of this book. However, when thinking about the littlest ones there are specific challenges and concerns that parents confront. There are many organizations that offer guidance and resources. These include the National Association for the Education of Young People (NAEYP) for information about the early childhood profession and where it is headed;[95] Child Care Aware for child care resources;[96] and the National Institute for Early Education Research (NIEER) for information about academic research initiatives.[97] Plus, there are local and international associations, and issue-specific and topical online chatrooms to explore as well. For those who like to begin with a book, consider *The Importance of Being Little; What Young Children Really Need from Grownups.* Author Erika Christakis asks the question, "*What's it like to be a young child?*" She discusses environments, play, relationships, communication, learning opportunities, and other topics as she thoughtfully explores that question, and provides answers that can help to support children's development.

○ **Y**oung scholars—the Davidson Institute offers "*free services designed to nurture the intellectual, social, emotional, and academic development of profoundly intelligent young people between the ages of 5 and 18.*" These services include consulting, an online community, opportunities to attend informal gatherings and connect with other scholars, and an ambassador program for volunteerism. The website also has resources for parents and teachers.[98]

○ **Y**oung at heart—there's something to be said for the exuberance of youth. Help children develop, sustain, and share enthusiasm for the wonderful opportunities that each day can bring. Ralph Waldo Emerson said, "*Nothing great was ever achieved without enthusiasm.*"

Zoom: What Matters

It may seem ironic that this final segment, about surging forward, appears at the end of the book. However, it's a good time to reflect upon all the messages herein about how to support children as they develop their strengths. Those who are not moving ahead are either going backward, or standing still, and although there may be a time and place for that, it's good to help children strive—to set goals, and to reach for them, too.

Zoom (Ongoing forward motion)

○ **Z**enith—it's commendable to reach upward and plateau, and then to continue to work and stay on top of things.

○ **Z**one—everyone has comfort zones but extending oneself means pushing *beyond* them. The Zone of Proximal Development (ZPD) is a concept that was first introduced by psychologist Lev Vygotsky almost a hundred years ago. The ZPD refers to that sweet spot wherein people feel both challenge and familiarity, and can advance to the next level with effort, and with the help they might need to scaffold their learning. That help might include hints about how to answer questions; constructive feedback about performance; guided practice; illustrations; making connections to previous experiences; and other forms of reinforcement or direction. Kids can think of the ZPD as their own *"I can"* zone, a place where they're right on the verge of a new, exciting learning adventure.

○ **Z**est—encourage children to exhibit zip and zing, and to be zealous!

○ **ZZZZZ**—then find time to rest, and to call it a day.

   (Or maybe not…)

"My alphabet starts with this letter called Yuzz.
It's the letter I use to spell Yuzz-a-ma-tuzz.
You'll be sort of surprised what there is to be found
Once you go beyond "Z" and start poking around!"
~ Dr. Seuss

Bibliography

ABC Ontario (Association for Bright Children)

Assouline, S. G.; Colangelo, N.; Lupkowski-Shoplik, A.; Lipscomb, J; & Forstadt, L. (2009). *The Iowa Acceleration Scale, 3rd Edition*. Great Potential Press.

Assouline, S.G.; Colangelo, N.; Van Tassel-Baska, J.; and Lupkowski-Shoplik, A. (2015). *A Nation Empowered: America Trumps the Excuses Holding Back America's Brightest Students*. Belin Blank.

Belin-Blank Center, College of Education, University of Iowa

Borba, M. (2018). *End Peer Cruelty, Build Empathy: The Proven 6 Rs of Bullying Prevention that Create Inclusive, Safe, and Caring Schools*. Free Spirit.

Borba, M. (2016). *Unselfie: Why Empathetic Kids Succeed in Our All-About-Me World*. Touchstone.

Brill, A. (2014). *Twelve Alternatives to Time Out: Connected Discipline*. CreateSpace.

Brainology—Program at Mindset Works Online

Callard-Szulgit, R. (2012). *Perfectionism and Gifted Children, 2nd Ed*. Rowan and Littlefield.

CABHI – Centre for Aging and Brain Health Innovation

Cavoukian, R. *The Raffi Foundation for Child Honouring*

Child Care Aware

Christakis, E. (2016). *The Importance of Being Little; What Young Children Really Need from Grownups*. Viking.

Clinton, H. (2006). *It Takes a Village: And Other Lessons Children Teach Us*. Simon and Schuster.

Cover, M. *Parenting.2.0, Online*

Covey, S. (2011). *The Seven Habits of Highly Effective Teens.* Simon and Schuster.

Cross, T. (2017). *On the Social and Emotional Lives of Gifted Children, 5th Ed.* Prufrock Press.

Cutchlow, T. (2018). *Zero to Five: 70 Essential Parenting Tips Based on Science.* Pear Press.

Daniels, S. & Piechowski, M. (2008). *Living with Intensity: Understanding the Sensitivity, Excitability, and Emotional Development of Gifted Children, Adolescents, and Adults.* Great Potential Press.

Davidson Institute

Davis, J. L. (2010). *Bright, Talented, and Black: A Guide for Families of African American Gifted Learners.* Great Potential Press.

Delahooke, M. (2019). *Beyond Behaviors: Using Brain Science and Compassion to Understand and Solve Children's Behavioral Challenges.* PESI Publishing.

Dell'Antonia, K. J. (2018). *How to Be a Happier Parent: Raising a Family, Having a Life, and Loving (Almost) Every Minute.* Avery.

Deneire, H. *Children Are Composers (Online)*

Dimerman, S. (2015). *How to Influence Your Child for Good.* Collins.

Dimerman, S. (2019). *Don't Leave, Please Go: What You (and Your Teen) Need to Know before Heading to University or College.* Publisher Production Solutions.

Douglas, A. (2015). *Parenting through the Storm: How to Handle the Highs, the Lows, and Everything in Between.* Collins.

Douglas, A. (2016). *Parenting Through the Storm: Find Help, Hope, and Strength When Your Child Has Psychological Problems.* Guilford Publishing.

Douglas, A. (2019). *Happy Parents, Happy Kids.* Collins.

Douglas, D. (2017). *The Power of Self-Advocacy for Gifted Learners.* Free Spirit.

Duckworth. A. (2018). *Grit.: The Power of Passion and Perseverance.* Collins.

Duke University's Talent Identification Program

Dweck, C. (2007). *Mindset: The New Psychology of Success.* Ballantine Books.

Eanes, R. (2019). *The Gift of a Happy Mother.* TarcherPerigee.

Eanes, R. (2018). *The Positive Parenting Workbook.* TarcherPerigee.

Engel-Smothers, & Heim, S. M. (2009). *Boosting Your Baby's Brain Power.* Great Potential Press.

Fiedler, E. (2015). *Bright Adults: Uniqueness and Belonging across the Life Span*. Great Potential Press.

Foster, J. *"Fostering Kids' Success" column at The Creativity Post*

Foster, J. (2015). *Not Now, Maybe Later: Helping Children Overcome Procrastination*. Great Potential Press.

Foster, J. (2017). *Bust Your BUTS: Tips for Teens Who Procrastinate*. Great Potential Press.

Foster, J. (2009). *Extracurricular Activities—The Encyclopaedia of Giftedness, Creativity, and Talent*. Sage.

Foster, J. (2009). *Parental Attitudes—The Encyclopaedia of Giftedness, Creativity, and Talent*. Sage.

Foster, J. (2009). *Teacher Training—The Encyclopaedia of Giftedness, Creativity, and Talent*. Sage.

Gallagher, K. & Steinhauer, N. (2017). *Pushing the Limits: How Schools Can Prepare Our Children of Today for the Challenges of Tomorrow*. Doubleday Canada.

Gifted Unlimited, LLC

Gilman, B. (2008). *Academic Advocacy for Gifted Children: A Parent's Comprehensive Guide, 3rd Ed*. Great Potential Press.

Gladwell, M. (2008). *Outliers: The Story of Success*. Little, Brown and Company.

Goertzel, V.; Goertzel, M.; Goertzel, T.; & Hansen, A. (2004). *Cradles of Eminence*. Great Potential Press.

Gordon, M. (2012). *Roots of Empathy: Changing the World Child by Child*. Thomas Allen Publishers.

Greene, R. (2017). *Raising Human Beings: Creating a Collaborative Partnership with Your Child*. Scribner.

Halsted, J. W. (2009). *Some of My Best Friends Are Books, 3rd Edition*. Great Potential Press.

Hanscom, A. (2016). *Balanced and Barefoot: How Unrestricted Outdoor Play Makes for Strong, Confident, and Capable Children*. New Harbinger Publications.

Hanson, R. (2013). *Hardwiring Happiness: The New Brain Science of Contentment, Calm and Confidence*. Harmony.

Hanson, R. *TED Talk—Hardwiring Happiness: The Hidden Power of Everyday Experiences on the Modern Brain*.

Hanson, R. & Hanson, F. (2018). *Resilient: How to Grow an Unshakable Core of Calm, Strength, and Happiness.* Harmony.

Harvard University's Center for the Developing Child

Heitner, D. (2016). *Screenwise: Helping Kids Thrive (and Survive) in the Digital World.* Routledge.

Horowitz, F. D.; Subotnik, R.; & Matthews, D. (Editors) (2009). *The Development of Giftedness and Talent across the Life Span.* American Psychological Association.

Hurley, K. (2015). *The Happy Kid Handbook: How to Raise Joyful Children in a Stressful World.* TarcherPerigee.

Hurley, K. (2018). *No More Mean Girls: The Secret to Raising Strong, Confident, and Compassionate Girls.* TarcherPerigee.

Institute for Educational Advancement

Jolly, J. L.; Treffinger, D. J.; Ford Inman, T.; & Smutny, J. F. (Editors) (2010). *Parenting Gifted Children: The Authoritative Guide from the National Association for Gifted Children.* Prufrock Press.

Kanevsky, L. *Tool Kit for High End Curriculum Differentiation (Online)*

Kaufman, S. B. (2013). *Ungifted: Intelligence Redefined.* Basic Books.

Kaufman, S. B. & Gregoire, C. (2016). *Wired to Create: Unraveling the Mysteries of the Creative Mind.* TarcherPerigee.

Kennedy-Moore, E. *Dr. Friendtastic, Online*

Kennedy-Moore, E. (2017). *Growing Friendships: A Kids' Guide to Making and Keeping Friends.* Aladdin/Beyond Words.

Kennedy-Moore, E. (2019). *Kid Confidence: Help Your Child Make Friends, Build Resilience, and Develop Real Self-Esteem.* New Harbinger Publications.

Kerr, B. & McKay, R. (2014). *Smart Girls in the 21st Century: Understanding Talented Girls and Women.* Great Potential Press.

Kids Now. www.kidsnowcanada.org

Klein, A. (2002). *A Forgotten Voice: The Biography of Leta Stetter Hollingworth.* Great Potential Press.

Kopman, N. *Music with a Purpose (Online)*

Kottmeyer, C. *Hoagies' Gifted Education Page Online*

Kottmeyer, C. *Hoagies' Gifted Education Page Online*

Lahey, J. (2016). *The Gift of Failure: How the Best Parents Learn to Let Go So Their Children Can Succeed.* Harper Paperbacks.

Lapointe, V. (2016). *Discipline without Damage: How to Get Your Kids to Behave without Messing Them Up.* LifeTree Media.

Letran, J. (2017). *Unleash Your Inner Superpowers: And Destroy Fear and Self-Doubt.* Healed Mind, LLC.

Luedtke, S. P. (2013). *The Mommy Advantage: How Having Kids Can Make You Happier, Healthier, and Wealthier.* Panamint Publishing.

MacNamara, D. (2016). *Rest, Play, Grow: Making Sense of Preschoolers (Or Anyone Who Acts Like One).* Aona Books.

Michalko, M. *Famous Failures* (Online at *The Creativity Post*)

Markham, L. (2012). *Peaceful Parent, Happy Kids: How to Stop Yelling and Start Connecting (The Peaceful Parent Series).* TarcherPerigee.

Markham, L. (2018). *Peaceful Parent, Happy Kids Workbook.* PESI Publishing and Media.

Matthews, D. *Going Beyond Intelligence Blog* (at *Psychology Today*)

Matthews, D. & Foster, J. (2009). *Being Smart about Gifted Education; A Guidebook for Educators and Parents, 2nd Ed.* Great Potential Press.

Matthews, D. & Foster, J. (2014). *Beyond Intelligence: Secrets for Raising Happily Productive Kids.* House of Anansi Press.

Matthews, D. & Foster, J. (in press). *Intelligence, IQ Tests, and Assessments: What Do Parents Need to Know? What Should They Tell Their Kids* within *Success Strategies for Parenting Gifted Kids: Expert Advice from the National Association for Gifted Children* (Edited by Jolly, J.; Ford Inman, T.; Smutny, J. F.; & Nilles, K.). Prufrock Press.

Matthews, D. & Foster, J. *Mindsets and Gifted Education: Transformation in Progress (Mindset Works Blog)*

McCready, A. (2016). *The Me, Me, Me Epidemic: A Step-By-Step Guide to Raising Capable, Grateful Kids in an Over-Entitled World.* TarcherPerigee.

McGinn, A. *Goodnight Sleepsite Blog*

Mendaglio, S. (Editor) (2007). *Dabrowski's Theory of Positive Disintegration.* Great Potential Press.

Montgomery, T. *Raising Entrepreneurs Podcast, Online*

National Institute for Early Education Research

NAGC – National Association for Gifted Children

National Association for the Education of Young People

National Mentoring Partnership

Neihart, M. (2008). *Peak Performance for Smart Kids: Strategies and Tips for School Success.* Prufrock Press.

Newman, S. (2017). *The Book of No: 365 Ways to Say It and Mean It.* Turner.

Oakley, B. (2017). *Mindshift: Break Through Obstacles to Learning and Discover Your Hidden Passions.* TarcherPerigee.

Olszewski-Kubilius, P.; Subotnik, R.; and Worrell, F. C. (Editors). (2018). *Talent Development as a Framework for Gifted Education*: *Implications for Best Practices and Applications in Schools.* Prufrock Press.

Ontario Education Equity Action Plan

O'Roarty, C. *Joyful Courage Parenting Podcast*

Peters, D. (2013). *Make Your Worrier a Warrior. A Guide to Conquering Your Child's Fears.* Great Potential Press.

Pfeiffer, S. (2017). Lessons Learned from Working with High-Ability Students. *Gifted Education International. 29(1), 86-97.*

Postma, M. (2017). *The Inconvenient Student: Critical Issues in the Identification and Education of Twice-Exceptional Students.* Royal Fireworks Publishing.

Price-Mitchell, M. *Roots of Action (Online)*

Price-Mitchell, M. (2015). *Tomorrow's Change-makers: Reclaiming the Power of Citizenship for a New Generation.* Eagle Harbor Publishing.

Prober, P. (2016). *Your Rainforest Mind: A Guide to the Well-being of Gifted Adults and Youth.* GHF Press.

Radcliffe, S. C. (2013). *The Fear Fix: Solutions for Every Child's Moments of Worry, Panic, and Fear.* Collins.

Radcliffe, S. C. (2009). *Raising Your Child without Raising Your Voice.* Collins.

Rey, H. A. & Rey, M. (2015). *Curious George Classic Collection.* HMH Books for Young Readers.

Renzulli Center for Gifted Education, Creativity and Talent Development

Rey, H. A. & Rey, M. (2015). *Curious George Classic Collection*. HMH Books for Young Readers.

Renzulli Center for Gifted Education, Creativity and Talent Development

Rimm, S. (2008). *Why Bright Kids Get Poor Grades and What You Can Do about It*. Great Potential Press.

Ruf, D.; Shroeder-Davis, S.; Hesselin, J.; & Keilty, W. (2018). *Chapter 14—Pathways to Supporting the Gifted: Four Educators' Personal Journeys* within *Nurturing the Development of GATE Teachers*. IGI Global.

Schafer, A. (2014). *Ain't Misbehaving*. Collins.

Schafer, A. (2014). *Honey, I Wrecked the Kids*. Collins

Schafer, A. (2014). *Breaking the Good Mom Myth*. Collins.

Schwarz, N. *Imperfect Families Blog*

SENG – Supporting Emotional Needs of the Gifted

Shanker, S. (2017). *Self-Reg: How to Help Your Child (and You) Break the Stress Cycle and Successfully Engage with Life*. Penguin Canada.

Siegel, D. J. & Bryson, T.P. (2012). *The Whole Bain Child: 12 Revolutionary Strategies to Nurture Your Child's Developing Mind*. Bantam.

Siegel, D. J. & Bryson, T. (2019). *The Yes Brain: How to Cultivate Courage, Curiosity, and Resilience in Your Child*. Bantam.

Skinner, W. (2007). *Life with Gifted Children*. Great Potential Press.

Stanley, T. (2017). *When Smart Kids Underachieve at School: Practical Solutions for Teachers*. Prufrock Press.

Steinberg, L. (2015). *Age of Opportunity: Lessons from the New Science of Adolescence*. Eamon, Dolan/Mariner Books.

Stiffelman, S. (2015). *Parenting with Presence: Practices for Raising Conscious, Confident, Caring Kids*. New World Library.

Tolan, S. Discovering the Gifted Ex-Child (Online) – originally appeared in *Roeper Review*, August, 1994.

Tomlinson, C. A. (2014). *The Differentiated Classroom: Responding to the Needs of All Learners, 2nd Edition*. ASCD.

Twice Exceptional Children's Advocacy

Van Donge, G. (2018). *The Cheetah Stories.* Royal Fireworks Publishing Co. Inc.

Van Gemert, L. (2019). *Perfectionism: A Practical Guide to Managing 'Never Good Enough.'* Gifted Guru Publishing.

Webb, J. (2013). *Searching for Meaning: Idealism, Bright Minds, Disillusionment, and Hope.* Great Potential Press.

Webb. J.; Gore, J.; Karnes.; & McDaniel, S. (2004). *Grandparents' Guide to Gifted Children.* Great Potential Press.

Webb., J. T.; Amend, E. R.; Beljan, P.; Webb, N. E.; Kuzujanakis, M.; Olenchak, R.; and Goerss, J. (2016). *Misdiagnosis and Dual Diagnosis of Gifted Children and Adults, 2nd Edition.* Great Potential Press.

Webb, J.; Gore, J.; Amend, E.; & Devries, A. (2007). *A Parents' Guide to Gifted Children.* Great Potential Press.

Weikle, B. *The New Family Podcast, Online*

Weinman, M. (2014). *It's About Time! Transforming Chaos into Calm, A to Z.* I Universe.

2E Newsletter

"*Don't cry because it's over. Smile because it happened.*"
~ Dr. Seuss

Endnotes

This is a list of links to online information sources relating to material noted in this book. These links were all active at the time of publication. Please be advised that URLs can change and, as a result, resource access may have to be adapted or investigated further in order to acquire the information.

1. Attitude—*Parental Attitudes—Segment Excerpted from The Encyclopaedia of Giftedness, Creativity, and Talent*—http://beyondintelligence.net/resources/

2. Access—*Hoagies' Gifted Education Page*—www.hoagiesgifted.org/gifted_books.htm

3. Access—*Resources Offered through Duke University's Talent Identification Program (TIP)*—www.tip.duke.edu/resources

4. Associations—*Listing of U.S. State Gifted Associations*—https://gifted.uconn.edu/stategt/

5. Above-level testing—*Information about Above-level Testing from Duke University's Talent Identification Program (TIP)*—www.tip.duke.edu/resources/advocacy-tools/just-facts-handouts/above-level-testing

6. Acceleration—*Information about The Iowa Acceleration Scale*—www.accelerationinstitute.org/Resources/IAS.aspx

7. Acceleration—*A Nation Empowered (The Ten-year Follow-up to A Nation Deceived)*—www.accelerationinstitute.org/Nation_Empowered/

8. Babies—*Zero to Three Website*—www.zerotothree.org

9. Behavioral problems—*Mona Delahooke's Blog*—https://monadelahooke.com/blog/

10. Behavioral problems—*Lives in the Balance Website—Collaborative and Proactive Solutions Model*—www.livesinthebalance.org/about-cps

11. Bullying—*Bullying Prevention*—www.stopbullying.gov.

12. Brain-based research—*Brainology Program*—www.mindsetworks.com

13. Character Education—*Roots of Action "Compass Advantage"*—www.rootsofaction. com

14. Competitions, Contests, and Clubs—*Johns Hopkins Center for Talent Development—Academic Competitions Resources*—www.cty.jhu.edu/resources/ academic-opportunities/competitions/

15. Computers and electronic devices—*Technology Doesn't Have to Be a Problem for Kids*—www.psychologytoday.com/us/blog/going-beyond-intelligence/201902/ technology-doesn-t-have-be-problem-kids

16. Computers and electronic devices—*Kiddle Online Search Engine* www.kiddle.co/ kidssafesearch.php

17. Creativity—*The Henry Ford Foundation*—https://www.thehenryford.org/ education/

18. Creativity—*Fostering Kids' Success—Joanne Foster's column at The Creativity Post*—www.creativitypost.com/authors/list/184/JFoster

19. Courage—Casey O'Roarty's *Joyful Courage Parenting Podcast*—www. joyfulcourage.com/jcp/

20. Differentiation—*Possibilities for Learning*—http://possibilitiesforlearning.com

21. Differentiation—*Renzulli Learning System*—https://renzullilearning.com

22. Dual exceptionalities—*2enewsletter*—www.2enewsletter.com

23. Dual exceptionalities—*Twice Exceptional Children's Advocacy*—www.teca2e.org

24. Direction—*Aha! Parenting*—www.ahaparenting.com

25. Emotional intelligence—*Children's Emotional Well-Being: 8 Practical Tips for Parents*—www.creativitypost.com/education/childrens_emotional_well_ being_eight_practical_tips_for_parents

26. Emotional intelligence—www.rootsofempathy.org/roots-of-empathy/

27. Empathy—*Michelle Borba's Parenting Blog*—www.micheeborba.com/blog/

28. Enterprise and Entrepreneurship—*Raising Entrepreneurs Podcast*—www. raisingentrepreneurspodcast.com

29. Enterprise and Entrepreneurship—http://julianeiman.com/blog/

30. Entitlement—*Amy McCready's Positive Parenting Solutions Blog*—www. positiveparentingsolutions.com/parenting-blog

31. Early entrance to college or university—*Johns Hopkins Center for Talent Development—List of Early College Entrance Programs*—www.cty.jhu.edu/ resources/academic-opportunities/college-entrance/

32. Extracurricular Activities—*Joyful Courage Podcast, Episode 63 on the Ups and Downs of Extracurricular Activities*—http://www.joyfulcourage.com

33. Extracurricular Activities—*Extracurricular Activities Segment in The Encyclopaedia of Giftedness, Creativity, and Talent*—http://beyondintelligence.net/resources/

34. Equity—*Education Equity Action Plan* for Ontario, Canada—www.edu.gov. on.ca/eng/about/education_equity_plan_en.pdf

35. Early Learning—*Deborah MacNamara's "Kid's Best Bet" Blog*—www.macnamara. ca/kids-best-bet-blog/

36. Flexibility—*How Children Learn*—www.rootsofaction.com/how-children-learn/

37. Friendships—*Dr. Friendtastic: Friendship Advice for Kids*—https://drfriendtastic. com

38. Findings—*Gifted Child Quarterly*—www.nagc.org/resources-publications/ nagc-publications/gifted-child-quarterly

39. Failure—*Famous Failures*—www.creativitypost.com/psychology/famous_failures

40. Family dynamics and values—*The New Family Podcasts*—www.thenewfamily.com

41. Family meetings—*Family Meetings Can Be Fun, Productive, and Meaningful*— https://www.rootsofaction.com/family-meetings/

42. Gifted: What Matters—*Lessons Learned from Working with Gifted and Creative Kids*—www.creativitypost.com/psychology/ lessons_learned_from_working_with_gifted_and_creative_kids

43. Gifted—*Johns Hopkins Center for Talented Youth*—www.cty.jhu.edu/about/

44. Hurrying—*The New Family Podcast, Episode 36 on A New Way of Thinking about Intelligence for a New World*—www.thenewfamily.com

45. Homeschooling—*Resources for Homeschooling Gifted Learners*—www. hoagiesgifted.org/home_school.htm

46. Honor– *Child Honouring*—raffifoundation.org/child/the-covenant/

47. Harvard—*Harvard University's Center for the Developing Child*—www.developingchild.harvard.edu

48. Hooray!—*Katie Hurley's Practical Parenting Blog*—www.practicalkatie.com

49. Integrity—*Compass Advantage*—www.rootsofaction.com

50. Kindling #6—*Good Night, Sleep Site Blog*—www.goodnightsleepsite.com/blog/

51. Kindling #7—*When Does Intelligence Peak?*—https://blogs.scientificamerican.com/beautiful-minds/when-does-intelligence-peak/

52. Even Keel—*Ann Douglas' Parenting Blog*—www.anndouglas.net/blog

53. Learning—*The Psychology Podcast with Scott Barry Kaufman: Episode 28, Learning How to Learn with Barbara Oakley*—https://scottbarrykaufman.com/podcast/learning-how-to-learn-with-barbara-oakley/

54. Links—*100 Resources for Gifted Kids*—www.notsoformulaic.com/resources-gifted-kids/

55. Life skills—*Parenting 2.0*—www.parenting2pt0.org

56. Lessons—*Seven Lessons for Modern Day Parents at Savvy Mom Online*—www.savvymom.ca

57. Mindfulness—*Mindful Website*—www.mindful.org/meditation/mindfulness-getting-started/

58. Music –*Appreciating Music as a Foundational Aspect of Creativity*—www.creativitypost.com/education/appreciating_music_as_a_foundational_aspect_of_creativity

59. Music—*Nancy Kopman's Music with a Purpose*—www.nancykopman.com

60. Music—*Hanne Deneire's House of Composers*—www.childrenarecomposers.com/platform-children-are-composers

61. Mentors—*National Mentoring Partnership*—www.mentoring.org

62. Mentors—*Mentorships and Kids*—www.creativitypost.com/education/mentorships_and_kids

63. Networks—*National Association for Gifted Children (NAGC)*—www.nagc.org

64. Networks—*Supporting Emotional Needs of the Gifted (SENG)*—www.sengifted.org

65. Nagging—*Imperfect Families Blog*—imperfectfamilies.com/blog/

66. Negativity—*Rick Hanson's TED Talk on Hardwiring Happiness: The Hidden Power of Everyday Experiences on the Modern Brain (How to Overcome the Brain's Negativity Bias)*—www.youtube.com/watch?v=jpuDyGgIeh0

67. Outings and fieldtrips—*Henry Ford Website*—www.thehenryford.org

68. Overexcitabilities—*Shout out to Barbara Kerr who shared her views and suggestions online. For a listing of her many publications, go to*—www.epsy.ku.edu/barbara-kerr#link3

69. Offerings—*Kids Now*—www.kidsnowcanada.org

70. Play—*YouTube video "Shake My Sillies Out"*—www.youtube.com/watch?v=WpuKbJgSgdM

71. Questions—*Sarah Chana Radcliffe's Parenting Posts*—www.sarahchanaradcliffe.com

72. Reading—*Want to Raise Smart, Kind Kids? Science Says Do This Every Day* –www.happyyouhappyfamily.com/raising-smart-kids

73. Reading—*"Good Books for Bright Kids" as suggested by John Hopkins Center for Talent Development*—www.cty.jhu.edu/resources/cty-reading-list.html

74. Resilience—*Quotes about Resilience that Foster Children's Determination and Self-Confidence*—www.rootsofaction.com/quotes-about-resilience/

75. Search—*Davidson Institute Database of Resources*—www.davidsongifted.org/search-Database

76. Spirited—*Going Beyond Intelligence*—*Dona Matthew's Column at Psychology Today*—www.psychologytoday.com/us/blog/going-beyond-intelligence

77. Thinking Skills—*Hoagies' Gifted Education Page for Kids*—www.hoagiesgifted.org/hoagies_kids.htm

78. Thinking Skills—*Critical and Creative Thinking Skills: The Joy of Learning*—www.davidsongifted.org/Search-Database/entry/A10834 *(Check the database and keyword "thinking skills" for more articles on this.)*

79. Technology –*Websites for Talent Development*—https://gifted.uconn.edu/schoolwide-enrichment-model/taledeve/

80. Technology—*Joanne Orlando's Blog on Technology Use*—www.joanneorlando.com.au/blog/

81. Talent Development –*Renzulli's Center for Gifted Education, Creativity, and Talent Development at the University of Connecticut*—https://gifted.uconn.edu

82. Talent development—*Belin-Blank Center, College of Education, University of Iowa*—www.belinblank.education.uiowa.edu

83. Talent development—*Center for Talent Development at Northwestern University*—www.ctd.northwestern.edu

84. Uniqueness—*Institute for Educational Advancement*—www.educationaladvancement.org

85. Untrained teachers—*Curb Your Complacency: Advocate for Gifted-Related Professional Development*—www.creativitypost.com/education/curb_your_complacency_advocate_for_gifted_related_professional_development

86. Untrained teachers—*Teacher Training—Segment Excerpted from the Encyclopaedia of Giftedness, Creativity, and Talent*—www.beyondintelligence.net/resources/

87. Vicissitudes—*Mindsets and Gifted Education: Transformation in Progress*—http://blog.mindsetworks.com/entry/mindsets-and-gifted-education-transformation-in-progress

88. Vicissitudes—Jacqui LeTran's website—www.jacquiletran.com

89. Xperience—*When Does Intelligence Peak?*—https://blogs.scientificamerican.com/beautiful-minds/when-does-intelligence-peak/

90. Xposure—*Discovering the Gifted Ex-Child*—www.sengifted.org/allarticles/discovering-the-gifted-ex-child

91. Xposure—*Resources on Adult Giftedness*—www.sengifted.org/allarticles/categories/adult-giftedness

92. Xecutive functioning—*Center for Aging and Brain Health Innovation*—www.cabhi.com

93. Xecutive functioning—*Baycrest Resources*—www.baycrest.org/Baycrest/Research-Innovation

94. Youth empowerment—*The WE Movement*—www.we.org/we-movement/

95. Young children—*National Association for the Education of Young People*—www.naeyc.org

96. Young children—*Child Care Aware*—www.childcareaware.org

97. Young children—*National Institute for Early Education Research*—www.childcareaware.org

98. Young Scholars—*The Davidson Institute*—http://www.davidsongifted.org/Young-Scholars

Acknowledgments

I pay tribute to Dr. James T. Webb who was my first publisher, esteemed colleague, and friend. He worked tirelessly in support of children's well-being. His efforts will continue to help families around the world through the reassuring messages he conveyed to individuals and groups; through the books he wrote and the many others he published at Great Potential Press; through SENG (Supporting Emotional Needs of the Gifted) the organization he founded; and through the words and actions of the thousands of people he mentored and encouraged. With this book, I honor his memory.

I'd like to thank Jennifer Jolly and Kathleen Nilles, the astute and proficient editors of NAGC's magazine *Parenting for High Potential* wherein the series "ABCs of Being Smart"—the original iteration of portions of this book—was published. Jennifer and Kathleen gave me latitude as I worked my way through the alphabet the first time around, one letter at a time...

I also want to extend my sincere appreciation to Christine Thammavongsa (Executive President of ABC Ontario—the Association for Bright Children). Christine's beautiful illustrations enhance the pages and cover of this book. I applaud her commitment, talent, insight, attention to detail, and creativity.

Publishing this book was an invigorating and collaborative venture, and I am grateful for the support of Molly Isaacs-McLeod. Her unwavering confidence in my work, her cheerful demeanor, and her willingness to trailblaze and to take leaps of faith kept me motivated throughout the process. I admire Molly's intelligence, resourcefulness, and determination.

Lisa Liddy is a gem among those who work in the publishing industry. She transformed my draft manuscript into this comprehensive, illustrated book, and she did so with efficiency and flair. I appreciate Lisa's expertise and finely-tuned design sense.

Diane Harris proofread the entire ABC manuscript slowly and carefully, looking for any possible errors. She would sometimes even send highlighted messages in the wee hours of the morning. I am grateful for her keen eye and dedication, but most of all I value her friendship.

I would like to acknowledge the many people with whom I connect professionally, my friends who have always been so supportive of my efforts, and all those individuals who have shared with me their thoughts, questions, concerns, and aspirations. These relate to children's development, giftedness, education, creativity, productivity, and well-being. I have listened, reflected, and researched these matters, and throughout these pages I've provided hundreds of ideas for moving forward. I hope these are helpful.

Eric, Cheryl, Michele, and Aaron continue to make me extremely proud and happy. It is gratifying to see how they and their young families are flourishing. I love all that they are, and all that they do.

Garry Foster is my guiding light. He is wise, kind, encouraging, and understanding, and he inspires me to keep pace with him as hand in hand we navigate the many intricacies, joys, challenges, and adventures of our lives. His love, and his ongoing faith in me, give meaning to every day. Thank you, Garry.

About the Author

Joanne Foster, Ed.D. is the author of *Bust Your BUTS: Tips for Teens Who Procrastinate* (winner of a 2018 International Book Publishers Association's BPA Silver Benjamin Franklin Award), and *Not Now, Maybe Later: Helping Children Overcome Procrastination*. She is also the co-author (with Dona Matthews) of *Beyond Intelligence: Secrets for Raising Happily Productive Kids*, and the multiple award-winning book *Being Smart about Gifted Education*. She has a Masters degree in Special Education and Adaptive Instruction, and a Doctoral degree in Human Development and Applied Psychology. As a parent, teacher, consultant, researcher, and education specialist, Dr. Foster has more than 30 years of experience working in the field of gifted education. She also taught at the Ontario Institute for Studies in Education at the University of Toronto for twelve years, where she took on the role of gifted liaison. She serves on advisory committees and advances community initiatives, and she presents on a wide range of topics at conferences and learning venues across North America. Dr. Foster writes extensively, including the column "Fostering Kids' Success" for *The Creativity Post* online, and she wrote the series "ABCs of Being Smart" which was featured in the National Association for Gifted Children's magazine *Parenting for High Potential* (and which provided the impetus for this book). Visit her website—and contact her—at www.joannefoster.ca

About the Illustrator

Christine Thammavongsa, B.A., A.O.C.A., is an illustrator, artist, author, product designer, and long time gifted advocate. She parented a gifted daughter, ran a home-based business, and during three decades as a design professional she applied her creative talents to home and lifestyle products, including merchandise for children. She has worked with dozens of well-known brands such as Dora the Explorer, Peanuts, Care Bears, Alice in Wonderland, Harry Potter, Beatrix Potter's Peter Rabbit, and a parade of classic Disney characters including Mickey & Friends, Winnie-the-Pooh, Bambi, Tinker Bell and all the Princesses. Thammavongsa now focuses on original illustration projects and gallery artwork to explore her artistic vision and creativity. She also serves as the President of the Board of Directors of the Association for Bright Children of Ontario (www. ABCOntario.ca), a parent support network which represents the voice of bright and gifted children while advocating for excellence in education.

CPSIA information can be obtained
at www.ICGtesting.com
Printed in the USA
FSHW011539100719
59859FS